The Amusings of a Missionary

a collection
of stories
from a missionary
to Japan

Ken Board

Published by
Citadel
A Division of Deep River Books
Sisters, Oregon

http://www.deepriverbooks.com

ISBN 13: 978-1-935265-31-3
ISBN-10 1-935265-31-8

Library of Congress Control Number: 2010933407

Printed in the USA

Cover design by Robin Black, www.blackbirdcreative.biz

Contents

Preface

If I were asked to enumerate my talents, I would list only one. My "talent" is the strange ability to do the wrong thing at the wrong time in the wrong place. This "talent" is responsible for many of the amusing incidents recorded in this book.

Every week I write a brief message for our church bulletin. Some time ago I grew weary of writing the same old boring messages that no one was reading and began writing about my own experiences and the experiences of my family, friends, and co-workers. It was never my intention to write a book. While laughing with me, and yes, at me, the members of my church learned biblical principles that became the basis of a Christian life fortified by the Word of God. The suggestion to share these incidents and principles in the form of a book came from them.

I wrote most of the stories with a smile on my face, but there are some that I wrote with tears streaming down my face. My prayer is that the experiences of my life and the lessons I learned through those experiences will be an inspiration to other Christians and provide a positive influence to lead lost souls to the glorious salvation that God has provided for all people through His Son, the Lord Jesus Christ.

Acknowledgments

Many of the stories in this book center around my family, my co-workers, and my church members. Their words and actions provided the ideas that led to these brief biblical messages. Although I have removed most of the names that appeared in the original messages, some of the people who appear in these stories will be recognizable to many of my friends. I hope my family will forgive me, I hope my co-workers will still speak to me, and I pray my church members won't fire me.

Also, I am deeply grateful to the staff at Deep River Books. I doubt they have ever received a "rough" draft that was any rougher than the first draft I sent them. They have patiently led me through the process of the publication of this book one step at a time. Their faith in me and their confidence that the messages in this book could be a blessing to others made *The Amusings of a Missionary* a reality.

THE AWFUL
GREEN BEAN CASSEROLE

Last week I enjoyed Thanksgiving dinner with a missionary friend and his family. His wife prepared a marvelous meal. There was turkey, mashed potatoes, cranberry sauce, pumpkin pie, and my favorite dish—macaroni and cheese. Also, there was a green bean casserole. As soon as I heard the "amen" to end the prayer of thanksgiving, I filled up my plate and began to gulp down the food.

Except for the green bean casserole, it was all delicious. When I tasted the casserole my first thought was, "This is the worst green bean casserole I have ever eaten." It tasted like paper. Just then my friend's wife said to me, "Brother Board, you're eating your napkin." I looked, and sure enough, there was a napkin underneath the casserole. I had been in such a hurry to start eating that I did not notice that she had already placed a napkin on my plate. I had covered the napkin with the green bean casserole and was eating them together.

If you can imagine the look on my face when the delicious food changed into that awful green bean casserole, you should be able to imagine the hearts of many people. When they look at the pleasures of the world, those pleasures seem delightful, but when they actually experience them, there is an awful taste left in their heart. A Bible character named Solomon wrote these words: "I said in mine heart, Go to now, I will prove thee with mirth, therefore enjoy pleasure. And whatsoever mine eyes desired I kept not from them, I withheld not my heart from any joy. Therefore I hated life: for all is vanity" (Ecclesiastes 2:1, 10, 17).

Tasting the pleasures of this world is like eating a napkin with your green bean casserole. However, a personal relationship with God and a deep knowledge of His Word will leave a pleasant taste in our hearts: "O taste and see that the Lord is good: blessed is the man that trusteth in him" (Psalm 34:8). "The statutes of the Lord are right, rejoicing the heart: More to be desired are they than gold, yea, than much fine gold: sweeter also than honey and the honeycomb" (Psalm 19:8, 10).

WHAT'S THAT SMELL?

One Sunday evening on my way to the Fukuoka airport to meet some friends, I became aware of a terrible smell in the car. My nose is not very sensitive, so unless the odor is quite a strong odor, I usually don't even notice it. But I noticed this smell and it was getting worse by the minute.

As I neared the airport, I was thinking, "What in the world is that smell?" It came to me suddenly. "Oh no, it's the church garbage! The church garbage is still in the car!"

On Sunday I usually take the church garbage home and put it out with our garbage the next morning. I had intended to take it out of my car when I took my family home before I went to the airport, but I forgot. Most people would have noticed the smell of the garbage right away, but with my insensitive sense of smell, I was well on my way to the airport before I realized that the garbage was still in the car. I had no choice but to meet my friends in my smelly car. I apologized to them over and over again, but the one-and-a-half-hour drive to their home was a miserable trip.

It could be that there is something "stinking" in our Christian life, something of which we are not aware but is causing the Lord to say, "What's that smell?" Our lives should be a sweet savor to the Lord, but if there is some habit in our life that is not pleasing to the Lord, the sensitive nose of the Lord will notice it right away. How terrible it would be to have the Lord speak to us the same words that He spoke to the people of Israel. "And it shall come to pass, that instead of sweet smell there shall be stink" (Isaiah 3:24).

If among our actions or hobbies or pleasures there is something that would cause the Lord to say, "What's that smell?" let's apologize to Him right away, and with His help, let's rid our life of that smell so that our daily walk will be a sweet savor to Him.

Ken Board

AMUSING GRACE

There is a Japanese pastor and his wife who have become dear friends to me. Every time I visit with them, I receive many spiritual blessings. We talk about many different things, but especially we talk about God and the Word of God. One night after supper we sat at the table and talked about the Bible for quite a while. When the subject became the grace of God, the pastor quoted the words of that great hymn "Amazing Grace." He tried to say the title of the hymn in English, but instead of "Amazing Grace" he said, "Amusing Grace." I couldn't help but roar with laughter.

On the way home I was still thinking about his mistake, but then I began to realize that certainly God's grace is amazing grace, but it is also amusing grace. When I checked the definition of the word *amusing* in the dictionary, the first definition that was given is "causing laughter or smiles." If this definition is correct, then certainly the grace of God is "amusing grace."

God's "amusing grace" makes us smile because it saves us from our sins (Ephesians 2:5–8). God's "amusing grace" makes us smile because it makes us righteous (Romans 3:24). God's "amusing grace" makes us smile because it forgives our sins (Ephesians 1:7). God's "amusing grace" makes us smile because it gives us a wonderful hope (2 Thessalonians 2:16). God's "amusing grace" makes us smile because it gives us help in time of need (Hebrews 4:16).

There are many, many other blessings that cause us to smile, so along with God's "amazing grace," let's also be thankful for His "amusing grace."

THE BLUE SOCK

On a hot Sunday morning I began to perspire during my message. I reached into my pocket to pull out my handkerchief to wipe my face, but it was not a white handkerchief that came out of my pocket. It was a blue sock. Of course, everyone laughed.

Do you want to know why I had a blue sock in my pocket? Let me explain. The reason is the pain in my foot (I have neuropathy). When I wear shoes and socks, my left foot hurts. Of course, when I enter church, I remove my shoes and put on slippers, but because my foot hurts even when I'm wearing just socks, I take off my left sock and put it into my pocket. Thus, when I intended to take my handkerchief out of the pocket, a blue sock appeared instead. I had hidden the sock in my pocket so it wouldn't be seen. However, at a time when I was not expecting it, the blue sock appeared in front of everyone.

The same is true of the sin that we hide in our hearts. We try to hide our unrighteous actions so they won't be seen by our parents, friends, husband, wife, or pastor. For a while, maybe even for a long period of time, we may succeed. However, according to the Bible, the time is coming when all of our sins shall be openly revealed. "Therefore judge nothing before the time, until the Lord come, who both will bring to light the hidden things of darkness, and will make manifest the counsels of the hearts" (1 Corinthians 4:5).

Therefore, let's examine ourselves daily and confess our sins, and receive God's forgiveness. "If we confess our sins, he is faithful and just to forgive us our sins, and to cleanse us from all unrighteousness" (1 John 1:9).

Ken Board

WHERE'S THE SPIDER?

If you watched me every morning when I walk out to get the newspaper, you would probably think I was crazy. That's because I always stop at the top of the steps and wave my cane around in the air before I go down the steps. Why? Because there are trees on both sides of the steps, and there is a spider living somewhere in those trees.

Every night the spider builds a web between those trees, so every morning when I start down the steps to get the newspaper, suddenly my face is covered with a spider web. Of course, the sensation of having a spider web across my face is not a pleasant sensation, but I'm not all that worried about the spider web. I am concerned more about the spider who built the web. As I check myself from head to toe, I shout, "Where's the spider? Where's the spider?"

It is terrible beginning each day with this spider-web experience, so I developed a habit of stopping at the top of the steps and waving my cane around in the area between the trees before I start down the steps. In no time at all, the spider stopped building its web there; however, just to make sure there was no web, for a while I continued my habit of waving the cane between the trees, but the spider web did not return, so I discontinued my cane-waving custom.

Several weeks passed. The other day when I started down the steps to get my newspaper, once again I felt that awful sensation of my face covered with a spider web. Once again my shouts echoed through the neighborhood. "Where's the spider? Where's the spider?" Because I assumed I had beaten the spider, I had become careless and once again was caught in the spider's web.

The temptation that comes from Satan is similar to that spider web. Just when we think we have overcome the sin that was troubling us, unexpectedly we end up caught in the Devil's trap again. Listen to the words of the Lord Jesus: "Watch and pray, that ye enter not into temptation" (Matthew 26:41).

Also, there is this warning in 1 Peter 5:8: "Be sober, be vigilant; because your adversary the devil, as a roaring lion, walketh about, seeking whom he may devour." Let's be on guard against the Devil, who sets his traps and waits to ambush us like a spider that builds its web and waits for its prey.

BROTHER DANIEL'S FISH

Brother Daniel and I went fishing with a Japanese pastor. The weather was great, and we could see a lot of fish in the water, so I thought I would catch plenty of fish. Even though the pastor, who is a very good fisherman, caught several fish, I caught only one fish in two hours of fishing.

Brother Daniel caught two fish, but he took only one fish home with him. When he lifted the second fish onto the dock, a cat that had been hiding nearby jumped out, grabbed that fish, and took off running. Daniel yelled at the cat and chased after it, but he couldn't catch it. The surprised look on his face when that cat grabbed his fish was so funny that I laughed for about ten minutes. On the way back to the church we saw three kittens eating Daniel's fish.

When I looked at that cat running away with Daniel's fish, I thought of false teachers and cultists who try to snatch the souls of men. Like a cat that steals a fish it didn't catch, these people try to steal the believers that other churches have led to the Lord. If they meet someone who is a Christian, they will visit the home again and again until they are able to persuade that person to leave his church and join their organization.

The Bible prophesied the appearance of these people. "But there were false prophets among the people, even as there shall be false teachers among you, who privily shall bring in damnable heresies" (2 Peter 2:1).

So let's be on guard lest we end up like Brother Daniel's fish. "That we henceforth be no more children, tossed to and fro, and carried about with every wind of doctrine, by the sleight of men, and cunning craftiness, whereby they lie in wait to deceive; But speaking the truth in love, may grow up into him in all things" (Ephesians 4:14–15).

Ken Board

THE BLACK PIZZA

My wife will return from America in twenty days, and because I don't know how to cook, I can hardly wait. Of course, there are many restaurants and fast food stores in this area, and before she left, Louise prepared a lot of food that just needs to be warmed, so it's not like I am going to starve to death. She left some frozen pizzas in the refrigerator, so I followed the instructions she had written for me and fixed one of those, and it was so delicious that a few days later I decided to have another one. However, this time, when I opened the oven and took out the pizza, it was black. I wondered, "What's going on? This didn't happen the last time."

The next day when my wife called me, I told her about the black pizza, and she asked me, "Did you put the pizza in the top part of the oven or in the bottom part?" The instant I heard her question, I knew what I had done wrong. When I fixed the first pizza, I read her instructions carefully and put the pizza in the top part of the oven, but when I fixed the second pizza, I failed to read her instructions again and confidently put the pizza in the wrong part of the oven.

When I followed her instructions, it went well, but when I ignored her instructions, I ended up with a black pizza. How closely this resembles the Christian life! When we follow the teachings of the Word of God, we are blessed. When we ignore those teachings, we stumble.

If our current Christian life is starting to look something like a black pizza, let's pay heed to the words written in James 1:23–25: "For if any be a hearer of the word, and not a doer, he is like unto a man beholding his natural face in a glass: for he beholdeth himself, and goeth his way, and straightway forgetteth what manner of man he was. But whoso looketh into the perfect law of liberty, and continueth therein, he being not a forgetful hearer, but a doer of the work, this man shall be blessed in his deed."

YELLOW PICKLES
AND WHITE PICKLES

Whenever I order a Japanese meal at a restaurant, usually pickles made from radishes are served with the meal, and most of the time the pickles are yellow in color. There are some pickles that I like, but I don't care much for the yellow pickles because they are hard and leave a bitter taste in my mouth.

One day when I was visiting my son and his family in Kagoshima, we decided to have supper at an *udon* (noodles) restaurant. Before the meal, our waitress brought us a small container of pickles. When I lifted the lid and looked inside, I saw that the pickles were the kind made from radishes. My first reaction was, "Pickled radishes. No thank you. I don't want any." However, these pickles were not yellow. They were white.

Until now I had never even seen, much less tasted, a white pickled radish, so I took one and smelled it. It had a pleasant smell, so I ate it. To my surprise, it wasn't hard like the yellow pickles. Not only that, it left a sweet taste in my mouth. That night, for the first time, I enjoyed eating pickled radishes.

If we compare our Christian life to pickled radishes, it should not be like the hard, bitter pickles but more like the soft, sweet pickles. "And the servant of the Lord must not strive; but be gentle unto all men, apt to teach, patient, In meekness instructing those that oppose themselves; if God peradventure will give them repentance to the acknowledging of the truth" (2 Timothy 2:24–25).

When we go out into the world and have contact with the unsaved people around us, through our words, our deeds, and our attitude let's leave an impression that is similar to the pleasant savor and taste of a white pickled radish. "For we are unto God, a sweet savour of Christ, in them that are saved, and in them that perish" (2 Corinthians 2:15).

Ken Board

CHEESE, CHEESE, AND MORE CHEESE!

I love spaghetti. At almost any supermarket I can find spaghetti that can be easily cooked in a microwave oven. The spaghetti already has meat sauce and parmesan cheese on it, but I always add a little more meat sauce and a lot more cheese. In fact, I put so much cheese on my spaghetti that you can barely see the spaghetti.

The parmesan cheese tends to harden inside the container, so before I put it on the spaghetti, I always shake the container vigorously several times. When I did that the other day, I didn't notice that the container was slightly open. The next thing I knew the table was covered with cheese. The floor was covered with cheese. My clothes were covered with cheese. Everywhere I looked there was cheese, cheese, and more cheese.

Because I didn't make certain the container was closed securely, my kitchen was filled with cheese. Likewise, when Christians go out into this world of wickedness, if we do not close the eyes of our soul, our heart will end up filled with all sorts of indecent thoughts and imaginations.

Isaiah 33:15 describes the characteristics of the person who will be able to escape the judgment of the Lord. "He that walketh righteously, and speaketh uprightly; he that despiseth the gain of oppressions, that shaketh his hands from holding of bribes, that stoppeth his ears from hearing of blood, and shutteth his eyes from seeing evil."

Much of the reading material and many of the TV programs and movies of this age are filled with evil. In order that this evil does not enter our heart and ruin our spiritual life, let's shut our eyes from seeing evil. If we don't, just as it was very difficult to remove all the cheese from my kitchen and my clothes, it may be extremely difficult for us to remove that evil from our lives.

In Psalm 141:3 David prayed, "Set a watch, O Lord, before my mouth; keep the door of my lips." Let's follow his example and pray, "Set a watch, O Lord, before my eyes."

TOO MANY ZEROS

Every year I have to notify the ward office of my estimated income for the year. The office uses that amount to determine the amount of my monthly payment to the national health insurance program. I wrote in the amount and mailed the document. A couple of weeks later, the office notified me of the amount of my monthly payment. I was staggered to see that it was nearly three times the amount of the monthly payment of the previous year. I mentioned it to some of the people at church and they told me that the health insurance had increased. When I told them that my payment had nearly tripled, they remarked that it may have increased that much because I had gone to the doctor so often the previous year.

A few days later when I had to go to the ward office on some other business, I found out why my payment had tripled. One of the clerks at the office handed me the document that I had mailed and asked me, "Is this your estimated income for this year?" I looked at it in amazement. There were too many zeros. I had filed an estimated income amount that was actually ten times more than my actual income. That's why my health insurance payment had tripled.

Normally the number "0" has no value at all, but when you add it to the right of a series of numbers, that zero increase the value of that number ten times.

The Bible teaches that those who are chosen by the Lord to do His work resemble zeros. "God hath chosen the foolish things of the world to confound the wise; and God hath chosen the weak things of the world to confound the things which are mighty. And base things of the world, and things which are despised, hath God chosen, yea, and things which are not, to bring to nought things that are" (1 Corinthians 1:27–28).

I have been told that the meaning of the phrase *things which are not* is "things less than one." What is less than one? Of course, it is zero. God chooses people who are zeros to do His work. However, just as adding a zero to the right of a series of numbers increases the value tenfold, when our "zero" is added to the power of God the Father, God the Son, and God the Holy Spirit, we become many times more powerful.

Ken Board

WALKING THE DOG

Every day it was the same routine. After supper I would go to the front door and put on my shoes. Then I would call my daughter to the door and help her put on her shoes. Finally, I would call the dog to the door and put the leash on him. Just before we left the house, I would grab my cane. Every day I went through the same procedure to take the dog for a walk.

One day I went to the door and put on my shoes, helped my daughter put on her shoes, grabbed my cane, and took off on our walk. We hadn't gone far when I embarrassingly realized that I had forgotten the dog. We were walking the dog without the dog.

Consider the routine of a typical Sunday. We get dressed, grab our Bibles, and head for church. Perhaps we are involved in some sort of ministry, such as teaching a Sunday school class or singing in the choir, or perhaps we go and just sit in a pew. We sing, pray, give an offering, listen to a sermon, and go home. It's the same routine every Sunday. We are diligent in maintaining our routine, but perhaps we are forgetting the most important purpose for going to church. That's our fellowship with the Lord Himself. In Philippians 3:10 Paul expressed three desires of his heart: "that I may know him, and the power of his resurrection, and the fellowship of his sufferings."

Even though we may follow our Sunday routine zealously, if we walk away from church without having come to know more about the Lord and His power, are we any different than a man who takes his dog for a walk without the dog?

"DID YOU BRING THE TUNA FISH?"

A couple of years ago we decided to spend the afternoon at the beach. The Sea of Japan is about a thirty-minute drive from our house, and we know an isolated spot where there will be no one curious to see the foreigners. When it was time for supper, I went to get the basket of chicken that my wife had prepared. I searched the car from one end to the other, but there was no chicken. We ate rice balls and watermelon and returned home to find the basket of chicken still sitting in the hall.

A few days ago we decided to go to the beach again. This time we were going to have tuna fish sandwiches for supper. I had not forgotten the fried chicken incident, so the last thing I did before I put the key into the ignition was to ask my wife, "Did you bring the tuna fish?"

She replied, "I already put it into the car."

My children and I played in the ocean for quite a while, and then about five o'clock we became hungry, so we left the water and walked over to the spot where my wife was preparing supper. When I saw her face, right away I knew she was upset. "What's wrong?" I asked.

She replied, "I brought the tuna fish, but I forgot the bread, so there won't be any sandwiches." We had watermelon for supper.

Something that I had been absolutely certain would never happen again had happened again. We can see the same occurrence in our Christian life. We stumble, but we promise ourselves that we shall never stumble like that again. However, as time passes, once again we stumble into the same trap.

The people of Israel stumbled in this way many times. Four times in the book of Judges the people of Israel "did evil in the sight of the Lord" and suffered greatly at the hands of their enemies. Four times they repented and called upon the name of the Lord and all four times the Lord sent a deliverer to free them from bondage.

When we commit once again the sin we had determined never to commit again, let us once again turn to the loving-kindness and tender mercies of the Lord and pray as David prayed in Psalm 51:1–2: "Have mercy upon me, O God, according to thy lovingkindness: according unto the multitude of thy tender mercies blot out my transgression. Wash me thoroughly from mine iniquity, and cleanse me from my sin."

Ken Board

THE SNOOPY LADY

I was standing at an ATM machine at the bank when a middle-aged lady appeared on my right side and began looking at the screen. I didn't appreciate the invasion of my privacy, so I gave her a look that said, "You're annoying me."

She ignored me and kept on watching as I continued with my transactions. I gave her a longer look which said, "It's rude of you to watch the ATM transactions of another person," and tried to block her view with my shoulder, but she continued to peer around my shoulder until I was finished.

As I turned to leave, she said, "Excuse me, but . . ." and in that instant she took a good look at my face and realized that I was a foreigner. She was speechless. Reacting to a hunch, I asked her, "Do you need assistance using the ATM?"

She replied, "Please." I stood beside her and guided her step-by-step through her transaction.

When she was finished, she said to me, "Oh dear. The instructions on the screen are written in Japanese, so because I am Japanese, I should have been the one to help you, but I had to have a foreigner help me. Oh dear."

Her words reminded me of a passage in the Bible. "For when for the time ye ought to be teachers, ye have need that one teach you again which be the first principles of the oracles of God" (Hebrews 5:12). A Christian who has been saved for several years should have grown spiritually to the extent that he is now able to instruct others in matters of faith. The words of the snoopy lady are appropriate for those who still need to have someone teach them. "Oh dear. Oh dear."

WATCH YOUR HEAD

I bought a new car, an eight-passenger van. My family and the church people liked the car, but vans weren't as popular then as they are now, so most of the church members had never ridden in a van. This presented a problem. Several of them banged their heads on the door when getting out of the van.

One young lady hit her head extremely hard, and I felt sorry for her, so I began warning her every time she got out of the van, "Watch your head." After a while these words became a joke between us. Every time she got out of the car I would say, "Watch your head," and she would reply, "It's okay. I'm all right."

The other day it happened again. As she was getting out of the car, I said, "Watch your head," and she replied, "It's okay. I'm all right." In the next instant I heard the sound of her head hitting the door. Even though it must have hurt a lot, she was smiling, and even though I felt sorry for her, I couldn't hold back my laughter.

As she stood there rubbing her head with a sheepish grin on her face, I couldn't help but think of people who ignore the warnings of church pastors. On a weekly basis the pastors warn them, "Watch out for your soul," but they think, "It's okay. I'm all right." Just as I couldn't help but laugh at the young lady who hit her head as she was saying, "It's okay. I'm all right," according to Proverbs 1:24–26, there will come a day when the Lord will laugh at those who ignored His warnings. "I have called, and ye refused; I have stretched out my hand, and no man regarded. But ye have set at nought all my counsel, and would none of my reproof. I also will laugh at your calamity."

What an awful experience it would be to stand before a holy God and hear His laughter ringing in our ears. Let's heed the warnings of the servants of God and watch out for our souls.

FIFTY MORE TRACTS
FOR A SECOND HELPING

One morning the pastor, one of the young men of the church, and I each took two hundred gospel tracts and passed them out from house to house. Our plan was to return to church for lunch, rest for a while, and then pass out two hundred more tracts apiece.

The pastor's wife had prepared us a delicious bowl of rice, chicken, and eggs. The young man quickly emptied his bowl and asked, "Are there seconds?"

Seizing an opportunity to tease the young man, the pastor replied, "Yes, but seconds will cost you fifty extra tracts."

As the young man contemplated the task of having to pass out fifty extra tracts in the afternoon when he was already tired, he told the pastor's wife, "Well, give me thirty tracts' worth."

As I laughed at the pastor's joke and the young man's clever reply, I was reminded of the parable of the talents in the twenty-fifth chapter of Matthew. "For the kingdom of heaven is as a man travelling into a far country, who called his own servants, and delivered unto them his goods. And unto one he gave five talents, to another two, and to another one; to every man according to his several ability" (verses 14–15).

There are various interpretations of this passage, but according to one interpretation, the man who traveled to a far country represents God and the three servants represent Christians who are serving the Lord. Just as the master of the house gave talents (money) to his servants, the Lord has given us "talents" (abilities and gifts), and just as the amount that each servant received was different, the talents that the Lord gives to us differ with each Christian. Therefore, it is a mistake to assume that the Lord requires the same work of all of us. If we have received two "bowls" of talents from the Lord, we have a responsibility to pass out two hundred and fifty tracts, but if we have received only one "bowl" from the Lord, two hundred tracts will be sufficient.

THE DAY I GOT MAD AT GOD

I t was the proverbial "straw that broke the camel's back." Earlier in the week there had already been a couple of incidents that didn't turn out the way I hoped, so that morning when I picked up my glasses and the frame broke, causing one of the lens to fall out into my hand, I lost my cool. I wasn't just mad. I was ticked. Do you know the difference between mad and ticked? When you're mad, you just think it. When you're ticked, you say it.

Well, I said it. I proceeded to tell God just what I thought of Him. Even if I could find a store that had a frame to fit my American-made lens, I knew it would be quite expensive. I have a friend who is an optometrist, so I went to the store next to his office and was told that there was only one frame in the store that would fit my lens. Without even asking the price, I ordered the new frame and went back the next day to pick up my glasses.

When the store clerk told me the price, I suddenly remembered something that had taken place just a few days earlier. The sister of the wife of a good friend of mine had been hospitalized, and since my friend is no longer able to drive, I drove him and his wife to the hospital several times and went with them to meet her when she was discharged. The next time I went over to their house, the sister tried to give me an envelope with some money in it. I refused the money several times, but they kept insisting until I finally accepted the money. The money in that envelope was just enough to pay for my new glasses!

When I realized that God knew ahead of time that my glasses were going to break and had already provided me with the money to buy new glasses, I left the store as quickly as possible and rushed to my car to be alone with the Lord. I apologized to Him for the harsh things I had said and asked Him to forgive me.

When we are upset with the Lord, let's be careful lest we are blinded by the circumstances of our life and fail to see the provision that the Lord has already made for our needs.

In the twenty-second chapter of Genesis, Isaac asked his father, "Behold the fire and the wood: but where is the lamb for a burnt offering?" (verse 7). In verse eight Abraham replied, "God will provide himself a lamb for a burnt offering."

The Christian must never forget that our God is "Jehovah-jireh" (verse 14), the God who will provide.

WHERE ARE THE BALLOONS?

The first time I went to a professional baseball game in Japan, I was quite amused at a custom that takes place in the middle of the seventh inning. In the top of the seventh inning everyone blows up long balloons, and as soon as the top of the inning ends, everyone stands and sings the team song and then they release their balloons. When the air is filled with the brilliant, whistling balloons, it is quite a spectacle.

Recently I went with another missionary to see a game at Yahoo Dome in Fukuoka. The home team won, so it was a delightful evening, but I left there with a somewhat sad feeling. As the top of the seventh inning approached, we noticed that no one was blowing up any balloons. I stopped one of the vendors and asked, "Where are the balloons?"

He replied, "We have temporarily discontinued the balloons to prevent the spread of the new type of influenza." I understood the team's decision to discontinue the balloons for now, but it just wasn't the same when the team song ended and everyone just sat down.

At the present time the government of Japan is utilizing every measure possible to prevent the spread of this new influenza. Also, many citizens of the country are being extremely cautious and wearing masks in order to protect themselves. However, according to the Bible, there is a "disease" much more dangerous than the new strain of influenza, a disease that has already spread to every person in the world. It is a disease of the heart called "sin."

Romans 5:12 clearly states that "all have sinned." In the same passage it is also written that "death passed upon all men." Many of the people who have been infected with the new flu have received treatment and recovered, but everyone who is infected with the disease called "sin" will die. We find these somber words in Ezekiel 18:4: "the soul that sinneth, it shall die." Also, in Romans 6:23 the Bible says, "The wages of sin is death." However, in the last part of this passage we find words that give us hope: "But the gift of God is eternal life through Jesus Christ our Lord."

When we believe in the Lord Jesus Christ and receive Him as our personal Savior, our heart is cured of this awful disease called "sin." "For God so loved the world, that he gave his only begotten Son, that whosoever believeth in him should not perish, but have everlasting life" (John 3:16).

GOD'S 7-11: "I'M GLAD IT WAS OPEN!"

Recently, a number of 7-11 convenience stores have opened in this area. When these stores first appeared in America, they were open from seven in the morning to eleven in the evening—thus the name 7-11. In Japan, too, the stores are called 7-11, but in Japan the stores are open twenty-four hours a day. The 7-11 company has conducted a brilliant advertising campaign on television using the slogan "7-11, I'm glad it was open!" At the time most stores were open only from nine in the morning until eight in the evening, so when a person needed to purchase something between eight in the evening and nine in the morning, they would go to 7-11. I rarely go to 7-11, but there have been a few occasions when I too thought, "I'm glad it was open!"

According to the Bible, God's 7-11 is also always open. Perhaps you are wondering, "God's 7-11? What's that?"

In Matthew 7:7–11 the Lord Jesus stated, "Ask, and it shall be given you; seek, and ye shall find; knock, and it shall be opened unto you: For every one that asketh receiveth; and he that seeketh findeth; and to him that knocketh it shall be opened. Or what man is there of you, whom if his son ask bread, will he give him a stone? Or if he ask a fish, will he give him a serpent? If ye then, being evil, know how to give good gifts unto your children, how much more shall your Father which is in heaven give good things to them that ask him?"

God's storehouse of blessings is always open. God doesn't answer our prayers only when we are at church. God will answer our prayers at any time, at any place. In fact, the Lord desires to give us "good things," so if your needs are not being supplied, don't blame God. In James 4:2 the Bible says, "Ye have not, because ye ask not." Whether it is a physical need or a spiritual need, let's knock boldly on the door of God's 7-11. When we do so, we shall find that God's 7-11 is always open.

THE "HOT" SERMON

On Mother's Day I preached in the morning at the Kitakyushu church and in the afternoon at the Amagi church. I used the same message at both churches—a message entitled "Sound Teaching for Ladies" based on Titus 2:1–5. When I preached the message at Kitakyushu, I didn't notice any unusual reaction to the message, but when I preached it at Amagi, there was a painful look on the faces of the ladies and they actually began to sweat.

As I watched their reaction, I thought, "Wow, the ladies at Amagi are under such conviction from today's message that they are actually sweating."

But then another thought came to mind. "When I turned on the air conditioner just before church started, maybe I . . ." I stopped the message and checked the remote control for the air conditioner. I had hoped it wasn't what I thought it was, but to my dismay, I saw that I had mistakenly turned on the heat instead of the air conditioner. The cause of the sweat on the brow of the Amagi ladies wasn't my "hot" message. It was the warm air flowing out of the heater.

Actually, we need to hear a "hot" sermon now and then, a sermon that so convicts us of our sins that we begin to sweat. In 2 Timothy 4:2 the pastor is instructed to "preach the word; be instant in season, out of season; reprove, rebuke, exhort with all longsuffering and doctrine." Reproof, rebuke, and exhortation are the three main purposes of the messages of the pastor, so the next time we begin to sweat during the pastor's message, first of all let's check the setting on the air conditioner remote control, and if that is not the cause of our perspiration, let's search our own heart for the cause of our reaction to the pastor's "hot" sermon.

WALLY AND WILLY

This is a story about two cats. The name of the first cat is Wally. Wally is my daughter's pet. Because Wally is our cat, Wally is given everything he needs. When he is hungry, he knows where his cat food is, so he goes there and eats. When he is thirsty, he knows where his bowl of water is, so he goes there and drinks. When the weather is cold or rainy, Wally has a soft, warm place where he can sleep.

The name of the other cat is Willy. Willy is a stray cat. Our daughter, who is sympathetic toward all living creatures except for spiders, felt sorry for Willy one day and gave him some food. Since that day, Willy comes to our house every day and sits under the kitchen window and begs for food.

We don't give Wally's food to Willy, but occasionally we do give Willy some of our meal leftovers. At first Willy wouldn't let me anywhere near him, but as he grew more and more used to me, he finally let me touch him. If we leave the front door open, Willy will try to come into the house, but since he is not our cat, we don't allow him in the house.

The relationship of our family with Wally and Willy resembles the relationship of God with those people who have accepted Christ as their Savior and those people who have yet to believe in Christ and receive Him as their personal Savior. According to the Bible, God "maketh his sun to rise on the evil and on the good, and sendeth rain on the just and on the unjust" (Matthew 5:45). Just as our daughter has mercy not just on her own cat but on all cats, the Lord "is good to all: and his tender mercies are over all his works" (Psalm 145:9). "He is kind unto the unthankful and to the evil" (Luke 6:35).

Unjust people eat the food that God gives them. Unjust people drink the water that God gives them. Unjust people breathe the air that God gives them. However, the people who are able to enter heaven and dwell with God are those who have been born again by faith in the Lord Jesus Christ and become the children of God. The Bible clearly teaches that "except a man be born again, he cannot see the kingdom of God" (John 3:3).

Each one of us ought to consider seriously this question: Am I a Wally that lives in the house or a Willy that cannot come into the house?

Ken Board

HALF OF A MILLION-DOLLAR VIEW

Mount Sarakura looms over Kitakyushu City where I live. Although I did climb the mountain a couple of times in my younger days, I normally take advantage of the cable car and ski lift to go to the top of the mountain. The view is spectacular. The evening view is included in one of three "million-dollar" views in Japan.

Recently, the cable cars were remodeled and the ski lift was replaced by a slope car, so when my daughter and her husband came to Japan for a visit, they wanted to see the improvements. The slope car was supposed to be completed already, but when we exited the cable car, we were told that the slope car was still under construction, so the only way to go all the way to the top of the mountain would be to climb fifteen minutes up a set of stairs. Because of my age, my bad legs, and, yes, my weight, I decided not to go all the way to the top that day. My daughter and her husband eagerly climbed the steps to see the magnificent scenery. Because my wife and I stayed behind, we could see only one-half of the million-dollar view.

The Christian should constantly be aiming for a higher level of spiritual growth, but on many occasions we end up settling for much less because of physical weariness or emotional pain. That's why it is important for our inward man to be "renewed day by day" through prayer, the Word of God, and fellowship with the Lord (2 Corinthians 4:16).

When the cares of this world weary us and weigh us down, we are no longer able to climb the staircase of the life of faith. As a result, we miss out on many blessings. In Proverbs 15:24 it is written, "The way of life is above to the wise."

Let's be careful to maintain the condition of our soul and spirit in order to keep on climbing up to the "million-dollar view" even when the cable car of our Christian life stops halfway along the way.

THE BRIGHT RED NAPKIN

When a Japanese missionary couple visited our church on deputation, I took them out to eat at a nice restaurant. After we finished our meal, I stood up and headed for the cash register. I noticed that everyone seemed to be staring at me, so I wondered, "Why is everyone looking at me? Maybe it's because I'm a foreigner, or maybe it's because they heard me talking in Japanese with the missionaries."

I paid for the meal and turned toward the door where the missionaries were waiting. They laughed and said, "Pastor Board, you still have on your napkin." I looked down and saw the restaurant's bright red napkin hanging out of my trousers. Now I knew why everyone was staring at me. With my face filled with embarrassment, I jerked the napkin out of my trousers and left the restaurant as quickly as possible.

When we imagine what others are thinking of us, most of the time what we imagine and what they really think are totally different. We judge other people by their faces, clothes, cars, or homes and imagine what kind of people they must be, and then when we come to know them personally, we discover that they are nothing like what we imagined.

When the people in the restaurant saw me leaving with a bright red napkin hanging out of my trousers, their evaluation of me was probably quite low. It's only natural for the people of this world to judge others by their outward appearance, but the Bible teaches a different standard to Christians. "In lowliness of mind let each esteem other better than themselves" (Philippians 2:3). Therefore, if you happen to meet me some day and see a bright red napkin hanging out of my trousers, please don't judge me just by what you can see.

Ken Board

WHAT'S MY CAMERA DOING
IN MY BOWL OF RAMEN?

When people from America come to visit me, I enjoy taking them to see the famous spots in Kyushu—for example, the hot springs in Beppu or the volcano at Mount Aso or the atomic bomb museum at Nagasaki. I also enjoy taking them to restaurants to eat food that Americans usually do not eat, such as *gyooza* (meat and vegetable dumplings), Nagasaki *chanpon* (noodles and vegetables), and of course, sushi and sukiyaki. I especially enjoy taking Americans to a ramen shop so I can take pictures of them trying to eat ramen with chopsticks.

I had just finished taking several such pictures one day and headed back to the table to enjoy my bowl of delicious ramen (not the instant kind that is sold in grocery stores in America). As I neared the table, my camera slipped from my hand and landed right in the middle of my bowl of ramen and splashed noodles and soup all over my clothes and the floor. I grabbed the camera out of the ramen as quickly as I could and was able to save the film, but when the soup hit the camera batteries, the camera started making a popping sound. I never was able to use that camera again. Cameras and ramen just don't go together.

The Bible teaches us that there are other things that do not mix well. "And what concord hath Christ with Belial? Or what part hath he that believeth with an infidel? And what agreement hath the temple of God with idols?" (2 Corinthians 6:15–16). Because of family relationships and workplace relationships, it is impossible to avoid association with those who are not Christians, but let's be aware of the danger in those associations.

I grabbed my camera out of the bowl of ramen, and although I was able to save the film, the damage to the camera had already been done. When we find ourselves sinking deeper into relationships that could have a harmful influence on our Christian life, let's pay heed to the words written in 2 Corinthians 6:17–18: "Wherefore come out from among them, and be ye separate, saith the Lord, and touch not the unclean thing; and I will receive you. And will be a father unto you, and ye shall be my sons and daughters, saith the Lord Almighty."

INSIDE THE TUNNEL

As I drove home from church on the Kitakyushu City Expressway, I was listening to a baseball game on the radio. If the Tigers won the game, they would clinch the league championship, so even though I am not a fan of the Tigers, I wanted to hear the dramatic moment when they won the championship. There was, however, one problem. There are several tunnels between the church and my home, so at the most interesting time of the game, my car entered a tunnel and I could no longer hear the broadcast. I turned the volume up as loud as it would go, but I still couldn't hear the game. I began driving faster, trying to get out of the tunnel before the game ended. When I finally cleared the last tunnel, I could hear the broadcast once again. The game wasn't over yet, so I was able to hear the championship moment.

There may be times in our Christian life when, because of sin, we enter a tunnel where we can no longer hear the voice of the Lord. Of course, the Lord still loves us and wants to fellowship with us, but as long as we are inside the tunnel of sin, we can't hear the voice of the Lord and He will not hear our voice. "If I regard iniquity in my heart, the Lord will not hear me" (Psalm 66:18).

Have you ever prayed and sensed that your prayer hit the ceiling and bounced back? Have you ever wanted to hear the voice of God and found heaven silent? Do you know what to do when you find yourself in this situation? Do what I did in order to hear the radio broadcast. Get out of the tunnel as quickly as you can. Confess your sins to the Lord and ask Him to forgive you. If you will do that, once again you will be able to hear the voice of the Lord and have fellowship with Him.

THE WEED KILLER
THAT MADE THE WEEDS GROW

There is an organization called Silver made up of retired people who hire themselves out to do odd jobs. The other day when a couple of them came to do my yard work, a lady said to me, "Buy some weed killer and spread it over the yard." I went to a large garden shop and told the salesperson what the lady had told me. I took the weed killer home and spread it over the yard. There wasn't enough to cover the entire yard, so I just spread the weed killer here and there.

Three weeks passed. One day I looked out at my yard and was amazed. The weeds were like a jungle! The weeds were especially tall in the places where I had sown the weed killer. In fact, the weeds in the places where I had sown the weed killer were four to five times taller than the weeds in the other places. What in the world had happened?

I could think of only two possibilities. When I relayed the words of the Silver lady to the salesperson at the garden shop, either I said the wrong words or the lady didn't hear me correctly. In any case, the weed killer that I sowed did not kill the weeds; rather, it made them grow. I have learned to be more careful when I sow something in the yard.

In the same way, it is necessary for Christians to be careful of the things that are being sown in our hearts. For example, are our companions sowing good seeds or bad seeds in our hearts? "Evil communications corrupt good manners" (1 Corinthians 15:33).

Also, there are seeds that are sown in our hearts through our eyes. Christians must be careful of the television programs they watch and the books and magazines they read. And there are also bad seeds sown in our hearts through our ears. It is necessary to be cautious of the music to which we are always listening.

If seeds that cause us to grow spiritually are sown in our hearts just one day a week, and seeds that interfere with our spiritual growth are sown in our hearts the other six days of the week, eventually our spiritual life will resemble a yard full of weeds.

WEIGHT DISCOUNT DAY

E very other month, when I to go to a nearby clinic to have the status of my prostate cancer checked, I enjoy the laughter of the nurses who are aware of my long struggle with my weight. When they call me into the exam room, they are waiting with the scale. When I see it, I make a frightful face as if I have just seen some sort of terrible monster, and they laugh. The day I finally weighed less than 100 kilograms (220 pounds) for the first time, every nurse in the clinic laughed when I yelled, "YES!"

One day I walked in and said, "You don't need to weigh me today. Just write eighty on my chart." They laughed. They always subtract a couple of kilograms for the weight of my shoes and clothes, so they laughed the day I said, "The clothes and shoes I am wearing today are very heavy, so subtract ten kilograms." The other day I could hear even the doctor in the next room laughing when I asked, "Department stores have price discount days. Don't you have any weight discount days?" No matter how much I joke around with them, though, the scale doesn't lie, so they always record the weight shown on the scale.

According to the Bible, our actions are weighed by God (1 Samuel 2:3). Even though we try to cover our sins, and even though we may be successful in keeping them a secret from others, God hears our words and sees our actions. "He that planteth the ear, shall he not hear? He that formed the eye, shall he not see?" (Psalm 94:9). Also, according to Daniel 2:28, "There is a God in heaven who revealeth secrets."

It will be no joking matter when we step on His scale. The scale will reveal the truth. God forbid that we should hear the awful words that were spoken to Belshazzar in Daniel 5:27: "Thou art weighed in the balances, and art found wanting." When God is the judge, there are no "sin discounts."

"GO AHEAD, MAKE MY DAY."

Two other missionaries and I were on our way to Nagasaki when we stopped at a gas station in a small town. A policeman standing across the street spotted us, crossed the street, and with a "go ahead, make my day" attitude said to us, "Let me see your passport or Certificate of Alien Registration." (When I am in Japan, I am an "alien.")

We all handed our certificates to him, and he opened them one by one, looked at the pictures, and then looked at our faces. He returned our certificates to us and asked, "Where are you from? Where are you going?" After deciding that our identification papers were legitimate and that we were not a threat, he told us, "Be careful," and left.

So far, in forty-one years of ministry in Japan, I have been asked to show my identification papers only this one time. I don't know what would have happened to me if I had not been carrying my Certificate of Alien Registration that day.

Just as the three of us had to identify ourselves to the policeman, some day all of us will have to stand before God and identify ourselves. According to the seventh chapter of Matthew, there will be people who will produce their good works as proof of their faith. "Many will say to me in that day, Lord, Lord, have we not prophesied in thy name? and in thy name have cast out devils? And in thy name done many wonderful works? And then will I profess unto them, I never knew you" (7:22–23).

There is only one mark of identification that God will acknowledge— the blood of the Lord Jesus Christ. "Having therefore, brethren, boldness to enter into the holiest by the blood of Jesus" (Hebrews 10:19). If you have never received the Lord Jesus Christ as your personal Savior and had your sins cleansed by His precious blood, I urge you to believe in Christ today, for His blood is the only proof of identification that God will recognize.

THE HAM AND CHEESE SANDWICH

"Nebuchadnezzar dreamed dreams, wherewith his spirit was troubled, and his sleep brake from him" (Daniel 2:1).

I rarely dream, but the other night, just like Nebuchadnezzar, I had a dream that troubled my spirit. (I wonder if the ham and cheese sandwich that I ate right before I went to bed had any connection with my dream. I wonder if Nebuchadnezzar had a ham and cheese sandwich right before he went to bed.)

In my dream I was visiting a famous tourist spot in Japan with three pastor friends. I don't remember any details except for the fact that there was one adversity after another until I finally awoke. What do you suppose God was trying to teach me through my dream? I can think of only one thing: don't eat a ham and cheese sandwich right before you go to bed!

Although there was a period when God spoke to men through dreams, in these days He provides leadership by two different methods. First, God provides leadership through the Holy Spirit who dwells in each believer. In John 16:13 the Lord Jesus said, "When he, the Spirit of truth, is come, he will guide you into all truth."

Second, God provides leadership through His Word. "All scripture is given by inspiration of God, and is profitable for doctrine, for reproof, for correction, for instruction in righteousness: That the man of God may be perfect, throughly furnished unto all good works." (2 Timothy 3:16–17).

Therefore, when you are seeking leadership from the Lord, don't try the "dream after a ham and cheese sandwich" method. Instead, read the Word of God and obey the voice of the Holy Spirit.

Ken Board

WALLY'S HELMET

Our cat, Wally, got into a fight with another cat and came home bleeding. We rushed him to a veterinarian who, after treating the wound, put a special gadget on Wally's head to keep him from licking the medicine off the wound. When I first saw the gadget, it looked like a lampshade to me. After looking at it for two or three days, it reminded me of the bonnets that mothers and daughters wore in the popular TV series "Little House on the Prairie." However, since Wally is a male cat, we decided to call the gadget "Wally's helmet."

Of course, Wally hated his helmet. Throughout the day he would beg us to remove it from his head. The vet had told us to bring Wally back in a week, but Wally was so pitiful that we took him back in five days and had the gadget removed. By the next day Wally had reopened the wound, so we had to return to the vet and have the gadget put on him again.

Wally just couldn't understand that his "helmet" was for his protection. As I listened to him beg us to remove it, I was reminded of the experience of the children of Israel. The laws that God had given them were for their own protection and blessing. In Deuteronomy 28:1–2 Moses told them, "And it shall come to pass, if thou shalt hearken diligently unto the voice of the Lord they God, to observe and to do all his commandments which I command thee this day, that the Lord they God will set thee on high above all nations of the earth: and all these blessings shall come on thee."

The time came when the children of Israel came to regard those commandments as a yoke that interfered with their freedom, and they rejected them just as Wally rejected the helmet that protected him. "And they rejected his statutes, and his covenant that he made with their fathers . . . and went after the heathen that were round about them" (2 Kings 17:15).

Let's learn from their sad experience and understand that the commandments of the Lord are not a yoke around our neck to restrain the freedom of our actions; rather, like Wally's helmet, they are God's method of protecting us and blessing us. "For this is the love of God, that we keep his commandments: and his commandments are not grievous" (1 John 5:3).

MY MEAL AT THE FANCY HOTEL

During my eight-day trip to the Tokyo area, I spent six nights at several churches in the area, and the other two nights I spent at a fancy hotel as the guest of a couple who had invited me to speak at their wedding. My first night at the hotel I decided to eat somewhere outside the hotel because I knew the hotel meal prices would be expensive. I walked around for a while but couldn't find anything I wanted to eat, so I decided that, even though it was expensive, I would have my meal at the hotel restaurant.

I went to the restaurant and looked at the menu, but there just weren't any dishes that appealed to me, so I left the restaurant. Just then I spotted a small convenience store in the lobby of the hotel, so I bought some orange juice and a sandwich and took it to my room. I must confess that I as I sat in my splendid room on the thirty-ninth floor of the fancy hotel and drank my orange juice and ate my sandwich, I had mixed feelings. After all, when a person stays at a high-class hotel, shouldn't he go ahead and spend the money and enjoy a delicious meal?

If you can imagine me sitting in the fancy hotel and eating the snack I bought at the convenience store, you should be able to picture the spiritual life of some Christians. According to the Bible, it is God's desire that our spiritual life be an abundant life. In John 10:10 the Lord Jesus said, "I am come that they might have life, and that they might have it more abundantly."

In spite of God's desire for us to experience an abundant spiritual life, I wonder if there are not times when, because of doubt or disobedience, we are trying to fill our hearts with the "husks" of this world like the prodigal son in the famous parable recorded in the fifteenth chapter of Luke. We find these words in verse 17: "And when he came to himself, he said, How many hired servants of my father's have bread enough and to spare, and I perish with hunger!"

In 2 Corinthians 9:8 we are told, "God is able to make all grace abound toward you; that ye, always having all sufficiency in all things, may abound to every good work." There is no need for a Christian to sit in his room and drink some juice and eat a sandwich when God has made it possible for us to live an abundant spiritual life overflowing with His great blessings.

Ken Board

THE CLEANING LADIES
ARE COMING!

Every time I saw this scene on television I would laugh. The husband gets up in the morning and is surprised to see that his wife has already gotten up and is feverishly cleaning the house. He asks her, "What's going on? Why are you cleaning the house this early in the morning?" She replies, "The cleaning lady is coming today."

Still confused, the husband asks, "But isn't the cleaning lady coming to clean the house?"

"Yes, but I don't want her to think that I'm not a good housekeeper."

Until now I have always looked at this scene from the viewpoint of the husband and laughed, but now that I am looking at it from the viewpoint of the housewife, I'm not laughing any more. I live alone and just can't seem to find the time to clean the house, so there are two cleaning ladies who come twice a month and clean my house. Sure enough, exactly like the housewife in the television sitcom, on the days when the cleaning ladies come at 9:45 in the morning, from about 9:15 I frantically try to straighten up the house. A couple of times they have commended my housekeeping, but if they were to come thirty minutes earlier some day, I am certain that they would no longer consider me to be a good housekeeper.

My mindset on the days when the cleaning ladies come manifests the proper attitude of Christians who are looking forward to the second coming of Christ. In John 14:2 the Lord Jesus stated clearly, "I will come again." This event to which all Christians should be looking forward is called "the blessed hope" (Titus 2:13). The Christian who is embracing the hope that Christ could come back today will cleanse himself. "Beloved, now are we the sons of God, and it doth not yet appear what we shall be: but we know that, when he shall appear, we shall be like him, for we shall see him as he is. And every man that hath this hope in him purifieth himself, even as he is pure" (1 John 3:2–3).

The Lord is coming! Let's examine our hearts and see if we need to do some cleaning before He comes.

I COULDN'T BE A JUGGLER

I haven't been to the circus for several years, but when I was a child, and even after I became an adult, I enjoyed going to the circus. To me the clowns were the most delightful members of the circus, but after I returned home, I tried to imitate only one person that I had seen at the circus: the juggler. I would take several balls and toss them into the air just as I had seen the juggler do in his performance, but eventually one or more of the balls would fall to the floor.

Although I had no intention to do so, recently I tried my hand at juggling again. After I went to get the newspapers (Japanese and English), I remembered that it was milk delivery day, so I tucked the newspapers under my arm and grabbed the four small bottles of milk. After I went back inside the house, I tried to hold the newspapers, the milk bottles, and my cane with my left hand while I locked the door with my right hand, but one of the bottles slipped from my grasp and crashed to the floor and shattered. It turned out to be quite a task to clean up the glass and the milk.

Of course, I should have first carried the newspapers to the sofa and left them there. Next, I should have carried the milk bottles to the kitchen and put them in the refrigerator. Finally, I should have put my cane in its usual place. If I had done these three things one by one before trying to lock the door, I wouldn't have ended up with a mess of glass and milk.

When our life ends up in a mess, the cause may be the same. We are trying to handle several problems at the same time, but because we are unable to do so, just as my floor ended up full of spilled milk and pieces of broken glass, our hearts end up full of anxiety and stress.

In order to avoid this situation, let's determine the order of priority for our problems and try to solve each one of them in that order. It is especially important for Christians to determine God's will for their lives and then be diligent in that one thing. The apostle Paul wrote, "This one thing I do, forgetting those things which are behind, and reaching forth unto those things which are before, I press toward the mark for the prize of the high calling of God in Christ Jesus" (Philippians 3:13–14).

Ken Board

NUMBER 6 AND NUMBER 9

When I went to the bank near the Kokura train station, I parked my car in spot number 6 in the parking lot right in front of the station. When I finished my business at the bank and returned to the parking lot, I went to the payment machine, pushed button number 6, paid the amount shown on the screen and walked to my car. To my surprise, although I had paid the parking fee, the bar blocking the movement of my car was still in the up position. In a somewhat angry voice I grumbled, "What's going on? I paid the money."

As I tried to figure out why the bar had not gone down, I decided to check the number of my spot again. When I did, I discovered the problem. When I first looked at the number of my spot, I had looked at it upside down. It wasn't number 6. It was number 9. I returned to the payment machine, pushed button number 9, paid the parking fee again, and went home. However, what I really wanted to do was to stay there for a while and watch the face of the driver of the car in spot number 6 when he realized that his parking fee had already been paid.

Of course, it was not my intention to pay his fee. It happened because I mistook number 9 for number 6. When the Lord Jesus Christ died on the cross and paid the penalty for our sins, it was no mistake or accident. That was the express purpose of His coming. His death on the cross was no mere event or coincidence; rather, it was God's intended plan for saving us from our sins.

The angel declared this to the shepherds the night Christ was born. "Fear not: for, behold, I bring you good tidings of great joy, which shall be to all people. For unto you is born this day in the city of David a Savior, which is Christ the Lord" (Luke 2:10–11).

I suppose it is okay to say that the Lord Jesus was "killed," but actually he voluntarily gave His life to pay the penalty of our sins. In John 10:17–18 Jesus said, "I lay down my life, that I might take it again. No man taketh it from me, but I lay it down of myself."

The Lord Jesus came to our world for the specific purpose of saving us from the penalty of our sins. "For the Son of man is come to seek and to save that which was lost" (Luke 19:10).

THE CHEESELESS CHEESEBURGER

I decided I wanted a hamburger for lunch, so I got out the frying pan, turned on the stove, and put the meat into the pan. All of a sudden, I remembered the delicious cheeseburgers that my wife used to make for me. "A cheeseburger! That sounds great!" I took a piece of cheese from the refrigerator and put it on top of the meat.

When it came time to turn the meat over, I became aware of my mistake. I had already put the cheese on top of the meat, so when I turned the meat over, the melted cheese would stick to the frying pan. As I stood there wondering what to do, the top of the meat was still raw while the bottom became blacker and blacker. Finally, I just gave up and turned the meat over. When I did, just as I had thought, most of the melted cheese stuck to the frying pan. I ended up eating a cheeseburger with almost no cheese on it.

That day I learned that there is a proper order in cooking, and if you do not follow that order, you end up with food that is quite different than what you had expected. This is also true in the matter of becoming a Christian. There is only one correct order. First, we admit our sinful condition and confess our sins to the Lord. Next, we believe what the Bible says about Jesus Christ, namely the fact that Jesus Christ is the Savior who died on the cross for our sins. Then we receive the Lord Jesus Christ as our personal Savior. After that, not in order to become a Christian but because we have believed in Christ and already become a Christian, we get baptized.

There are some people who think that a person becomes a Christian by being baptized. For example, now and then when I ask a person, "When did you become a Christian?" they reply by telling me when they were baptized. Whenever I hear that reply, I wonder if that person really understands the method of becoming a Christian. Getting baptized in order to become a Christian is like putting the cheese on the hamburger before you turn it over.

"And as they went on their way, they came unto a certain water: and the eunuch said, 'See, here is water; what doth hinder me to be baptized?' And Philip said, 'If thou believest with all thine heart, thou mayest'" (Acts 8:36–37).

Repentance, faith in Christ, and then baptism—this is the correct order.

Ken Board

"I LEARNED HOW TO DRIVE LIKE THIS FROM THE JAPANESE!"

I was traveling on the Fukuoka City Expressway when I noticed a police car in my rearview mirror. For a second my heart began to beat faster, but I calmed myself down with these words: "I'm not doing anything wrong. I am driving safely. The police car is not chasing me."

When the police car pulled alongside me, suddenly I heard these words from the speaker on top of the police car: "Slow down. The speed limit on this road is sixty kilometers an hour." I looked at my speedometer. I was doing eighty, so I slowed down to sixty.

After the police car went on ahead, I yelled, "I learned how to drive like this from the Japanese!" This is true. When I first came to Japan, I observed the speed limit, but other cars went flying by me one after another. Gradually, I began driving over the speed limit like the other drivers. For example, the speed limit on the city expressway is sixty, but everyone drives at least eighty, so now I do too.

When I yelled, "I learned how to drive like this from the Japanese!" the Japanese pastor riding in the car with me said, "So because everyone else is doing it, you will do it too, huh?

I shot back, "Be quiet," but I began to feel guilty because I knew he was speaking the truth.

My "everyone else is doing it, so I will too" attitude reflects the way of thinking of many people. They know what they are doing is wrong, so they convince themselves that it is okay because everyone else is doing the same thing. However, this is not a good attitude for a Christian. Our conduct should be based upon the teachings of the Word of God, not the conduct of the people around us. "Be not conformed to this world" (Romans 12:2).

ONE WORD RUINED MY MESSAGE

I was teaching the Bible one Wednesday night at the Kitakyushu church when I decided to use an illustration about an American cowboy. This cowboy used to ride into town every weekend, tie his horse up in front of the saloon, and go in and get drunk. One day the cowboy became a Christian, so on Sunday he rode into town, tied his horse up in front of the saloon, but then went to the church. One of the church members who saw this admonished him. "Now that you are a Christian, you shouldn't tie your horse up in front of the saloon anymore." Through this illustration I was trying to make the point that when we become Christians, our lives should change.

One word ruined the illustration and my message that night. Instead of using the word *uma*, I used the word *tsuma*, so instead of saying, "The cowboy rode his horse into town and tied it up in front of the saloon," I said, "The cowboy rode his wife into town and tied her up in front of the saloon."

Normally, when I make a mistake in my Japanese, the church people are kind enough not to laugh at me, but this mistake was too much even for them. No one laughed out loud, but I could see several people giggling and trying to hold back the laughter. I continued the message for five more minutes but saw that it was useless to continue any longer. I ended the lesson and prayed. The instant I said "Amen," the entire church broke out into a roar of laughter.

It takes only one word to ruin a serious message. That's why I am thankful for the purity and perfection of the Bible. If there were even one mistake in the Bible, it could have serious consequences in our spiritual life, but praise be to God, His Word is perfect and pure. "The words of the Lord are pure words" (Psalm 12:6). "The law of the Lord is perfect" (Psalm 19:7). "Every word of God is pure" (Proverbs 30:5). In fact, in Matthew 5:18 the Lord Jesus declared, "Till heaven and earth pass, one jot or one tittle shall in no wise pass from the law."

I could fill this book with mistakes in the language that I and other missionaries have made, but as for the Word of God that we declare, there are no mistakes in it. Hallelujah!

Ken Board

MY VIEW FROM FLOOR 39

I traveled to Yokohama at the request of the bride to deliver the message at her wedding. The bride and groom reserved a room for me at a first-class hotel right by the train station. There are thirty-nine floors in this hotel, and my room was on the top floor. When I entered the room, the first thing I did was walk to the window and look down. As I did, three thoughts crossed my mind.

First, I thought, "What a magnificent view!"

Second, as I considered the distance to the ground, I remembered the experiences of people trapped in tall buildings by fires or earthquakes in some of the disaster movies I had seen and I sensed a slight feeling of fear.

It was the third thought that dominated my mind. As I looked down on the small images of people scurrying here and there, I wondered, "What are their names? What are their destinations and their plans? What are the worries that fill their hearts?"

In Isaiah 40:22 the Bible says this about God, "He sitteth upon the circle of the earth, and the inhabitants thereof are as grasshoppers." As I looked down upon people who seemed as small as grasshoppers, I knew nothing about them, but the God who sits on the circle of the earth and looks down upon mankind knows everything about us. He knows our names (John 10:3). He knows our sitting down and our rising up and understands our thoughts (Psalm 139:2). He knows our hearts (Acts 1:24).

How wonderful is the love of this God who takes a personal interest in each one of us! David expressed the same thought in these words, "What is man, that thou art mindful of him?" (Psalm 8:4). If God is this concerned for each one of us, how could anyone possibly be indifferent to the great love of this wonderful God! If He cares for us to this extent, let us respond with worship, service, and a way of living that pleases Him.

THE $9,000 PRAYER

Our Sunday morning service starts at 11:00, so I try to arrive at the church about 10:15. One Sunday morning when I arrived at church, I opened the back door of my car to take out my briefcase, but it wasn't there. I frantically searched the car several times, but I couldn't find the briefcase anywhere. When I realized that the briefcase wasn't in the car, my mind was filled with panic and hopelessness. I thought, "This can't be happening!" The money for the security deposit on our new building plus two months' rent was in that briefcase. Altogether it came to $9,000!

I jumped into the car and drove like a madman toward my home (it's a thirty-minute drive). As I drove, I prayed the same fervent prayer over and over again: "Lord, please protect the $9,000. Lord, please protect the $9,000."

When I arrived at the house, the briefcase was still sitting in the driveway right where I had left it. I arrived at church thirty minutes late, but the $9,000 was safe. My driveway is an open driveway, so anyone passing by my house could have seen the briefcase and taken it. I am confident that the briefcase was still there because the Lord heard my prayer and protected it. However, I am also aware of the fact that God's answer to my prayer was not related to the amount of the money.

According to the Bible, if our prayer is a $9,000 prayer or a one-cent prayer, the Lord will hear the fervent prayer of a righteous man (James 5:16). In fact, the Bible teaches us that the Lord will hear and answer any prayer that pleases Him. "And this is the confidence that we have in him, that, if we ask anything according to his will, he heareth us" (1 John 5:14).

There are times when we have to pray $9,000 prayers, and there are times when we pray less expensive prayers. Both kinds will be heard by the Lord when our request is according to His will.

Ken Board

WALLY AND CROSBY

We have a puppy at our house now. It's a Beagle named Crosby that someone gave to my son. Crosby has two favorite pastimes. One is gnawing on things. Crosby will gnaw on anything he can reach. His other favorite pastime is playing with our cat, Wally. When Crosby and Wally are playing, it is a sight to see. For a while Crosby will chase Wally around the house. When Wally grows tired of this game, he will turn and face Crosby. Crosby will pretend to bite Wally, and Wally will rake his claws over Crosby's nose. Crosby will let out a painful yelp and back up, but he's a tenacious puppy, so after a few seconds, he will head for Wally again. No matter how many times Wally scratches him with his claws, Crosby will soon go after Wally again.

When Wally has had enough, he will climb up to some spot where Crosby can't reach him. Crosby will howl and beg Wally to come down and play with him, but Wally just ignores Crosby and settles down for a nap in his place of refuge.

From time to time Christians will meet with similar experiences. As we fight a spiritual battle with a tenacious enemy, our soul and spirit become exhausted. When we feel that we just can't endure any longer, let's follow the example of Wally and go to a high place where our enemy can't reach us. That "high place" where we are safe from the attacks of the enemy is God's throne of grace. "Let us therefore come boldly unto the throne of grace, that we may obtain mercy, and find grace to help in time of need" (Hebrews 4:16).

When we read the Gospels, we see that the Lord Jesus went often to that "high place." For example, in Matthew 14:23 it is written, "And when he had sent the multitudes away, he went up into a mountain apart to pray." We can see the Lord going to that "high place" also in the first chapter of Mark, and in the fifth, sixth, and ninth chapters of Luke.

When we undergo the constant attacks of the enemy and draw close to the limit of our endurance, let's take refuge in our Savior who spoke these words that give us peace and hope. "Come unto me, all ye that labor and are heavy laden, and I will give you rest" (Matthew 11:28).

THE FUNNY BUMPER STICKER

I enjoy reading funny bumper stickers. For a while the bumper sticker, "Honk if you love Jesus" was popular, but the one that I liked said, "If you love Jesus, tithe. Anyone can honk." Here are some more of my favorites: Driver Carries No Cash. He's Married.

Honk If Anything Falls Off

Ever Stop to Think And Forget to Start Again?

Are You Following Jesus This Close?

Of All the Things I Lost, I Miss My Mind the Most

The other day I saw a funny bumper sticker on the car in front of me. It read "I observe the speed limit." Why was it funny? I was on the expressway headed toward church when I saw this car. The speed limit on that road is sixty kilometers an hour. The car with the "I observe the speed limit" bumper sticker was traveling at the speed of eighty kilometers an hour.

It is a simple thing to confess orally our faith in Christ, but it is our daily behavior that becomes the proof of our confession of faith. When our words and our conduct contradict each other, we too will become objects of laughter to the people around us.

James wrote these well-known words: "Show me thy faith without thy works, and I will shew thee my faith by my works" (James 2:18).

Also, in 1 John 1:6 the Bible says, "If we say that we have fellowship with him, and walk in darkness, we lie, and do not the truth."

Therefore, with the help of the Lord, let's make it our goal to demonstrate a lifestyle that is suitable to the confession of our mouth.

Ken Board

"PASTOR BOARD, PASTOR BOARD"

Whenever I go to the Kitakyushu church, the pastor's four-year-old daughter runs to the door to greet me with a big smile on her face because she thinks that I have come to the church just to play with her. Actually, I go there to teach an English class after the ladies' meeting, but she doesn't think so.

As soon as the English class is over she will come and tap me on the arm and say, "Pastor Board, Pastor Board," to get my attention. She never says "Pastor Board" just once. Without fail, she says it twice: "Pastor Board, Pastor Board."

If I do not stop talking with the adults and answer her within two or three seconds, she taps my arm again and repeats, "Pastor Board, Pastor Board." In fact, until I stop talking with the pastor and the ladies and play with her, she will continue to tap my arm and say, "Pastor Board, Pastor Board" every few seconds.

Christians could learn the correct way of praying from that little girl. In Matthew 7:7 the Lord Jesus said, "Ask, and it shall be given you; seek, and ye shall fine; knock, and it shall be opened unto you: For every one that asketh receiveth; and he that seeketh findeth; and to him that knocketh it shall be opened."

I have read that the verbs in this passage show continuous action, so we could read the passage like this: "Continue to ask, and it shall be given to you; continue to seek, and ye shall find; continue to knock, and it shall be opened unto you. For every one that continues to ask shall receive; and he that continues to seek shall find; and to him that continues to knock it shall be opened."

Like that little girl who keeps tapping on my arm and saying, "Pastor Board, Pastor Board" until I play with her, let's continue to call on the name of the Lord in prayer.

"Continue in prayer" (Colossians 4:2). "Continuing instant in prayer" (Romans 12:12).

THE DEAD DRAGONFLY

On the island of Nagashima in Kagoshima Prefecture there is a church surrounded by woods and fields. Usually, when someone is at the church during the summer, the front door is left open, and many different species of insects fly into the church.

One summer when I visited the church with a pastor friend and his family and a missionary friend and his family, their children were fascinated by the many different kinds of insects. They ran around trying to catch the insects with a net they had found. Suddenly, their shouts of joy changed into shouts of fear. They came running toward me screaming at the top of their lungs. Chasing behind them came one of the boys holding a large dragonfly in his hand. All of the children, especially the girls, were desperately trying to get away from that dragonfly.

I looked at the dragonfly for a few seconds and then began to laugh. The dragonfly was dead. They children were running away in fear from a dead dragonfly that could not hurt them.

As I sat there and watched them, it seemed that I could see the image of some Christians. In Romans 6:6–7 it is written, "Knowing this, that our old man is crucified with him, that the body of sin might be destroyed, that henceforth we should not serve sin. For he that is dead is freed from sin." When a person receives Jesus Christ as his personal Savior, he becomes a person who has been crucified with Christ and therefore is no longer under the domination of sin. What a wonderful truth! We are dead to sin and can now live a life of victory, so there is no need to live a spiritual life that resembles children running away in fear from a dead dragonfly.

"Likewise reckon ye also yourselves to be dead indeed to sin, but alive unto God through Jesus Christ our Lord" (Romans 6:11).

Ken Board

WHERE'S THE JAM?

Maybe it's because I am such an impatient person, but there are two things that are difficult for me. One is opening things wrapped in plastic or cellophane paper. I watch others pick up a cookie wrapped in cellophane and open it instantly, but when I try to open my cookie, it's a struggle. I tear at all four sides of the cookie until finally someone has mercy on me and opens it for me. It's a regular occurrence at church for one of the members to see me struggling to open something and say, "Pastor, give it to me. I'll open it for you."

One more difficult thing for me is finding things. I know where everything is in my office, but when I step into any other room in the house, I can't seem to find anything for which I am looking. Usually, I have to ask my wife to find it for me.

The other day I opened the refrigerator to look for some jam to put on my toast. First, I searched the four big shelves in the refrigerator. Next, I searched the five shelves on the door of the refrigerator. There was no jam anywhere. Finally, I gave up and asked my wife, "Where's the jam?"

She replied, "It's on the small shelf between the fourth shelf and the fifth shelf on the door." I bent over and looked, and, sure enough, there was a small shelf between the fourth shelf and the fifth shelf, and just as my wife had said, the jam was on that shelf. As long as I was standing, I couldn't see that small shelf. I had to bend down in order to see it.

The grace that God gives to us is similar to the jam on that small shelf. In James 4:6 and also in 1 Peter 5:7 the Bible says, "God resisteth the proud, but giveth grace unto the humble." As long as we stand in our pride and our vanity, God will not give us His grace, but when we acknowledge our weakness and our sins and humble ourselves before the Lord, He will answer our prayers and give us His grace. The parable of the Pharisee and the publican in Luke 18:9–14 makes this truth clear.

If we desire the Lord to put the jam of His grace on the toast of our life, we'll find that jam when we search for it with a heart that is bowed in humility.

"I SWAM"

My daughter entered the room and said, "Daddy, please take us to the park," so I loaded her and three of her friends into the car and drove to the park. It was a beautiful day, and many children were playing in the park. In fact, there were about as twice as many as usual. Foreigners are scare in this area, so as soon as the children saw me, they gathered around me with excitement. I had planned to read a book while my daughter was playing with her friends, but I ended up answering question after question.

One child asked me, "How did you come to Japan?" I jokingly answered, "I swam."

Of course, most of the children had a doubtful look on their faces, but one first-grade boy's eyes grew quite large and he exclaimed, "You swam? Wow!" When I realized that he really believed me, I told him the truth right away.

I couldn't help but laugh at the gullibility of that little boy, but at the same time I sensed the need of speaking the truth to people who are quick to believe everything they hear. In Matthew 18:3–6 the Lord Jesus spoke these well-known words: "Verily I say unto you, Except ye be converted and become as little children, ye shall not enter into the kingdom of heaven. Whosoever therefore shall humble himself as this little child, the same is greatest in the kingdom of heaven. And whoso shall receive one such little child in my name receiveth me. But whoso shall offend one of these little ones which believe in me, it were better for him that a millstone were hanged about his neck, and that he were drowned in the depth of the sea."

Public school teachers, private school teachers, Sunday school teachers, and, yes, parents too must be aware of the tremendous responsibility of their position and be careful of any action or words that might cause a child to stumble.

Ken Board

ROCK, SCISSORS, PAPER

Whenever I go to the Kitakyushu church, the pastor's little daughter wants me to play Rock, Scissors, Paper with her. She always puts out Rock, so I put out Paper and win. In order to make her smile, once in a while I will put out Scissors and let her win. She really enjoys it when I put out Rock too. When that happens, while shouting, "It's a tie," we change our hands. Of course, she puts out Rock again, so in order to keep the game going, I put out Rock again too. When this happens several times in a row, she starts giggling loudly. I love to watch her face when she's giggling, so I keep the game going as long as I can.

The other day when I went to the church, she was wearing her father's sweater. Immediately she wanted to play Rock, Scissors, Paper. Of course, she put out Rock, so I put out Paper. The sleeves of her father's sweater were longer than her arms, so her hands were hidden inside the sweater. After she saw that I had put out Paper, inside the sweater she changed from Rock to Scissors and beat me. She used this strategy to win every game that day.

Her strategy reminded me of the strategy used by the Devil to tempt Christians. The Devil shows sin as something delightful that can make us happy, but he hides the results of sin. For example, in the garden of Eden, he tricked Eve into believing that the forbidden fruit was good for food and desirable to make one wise (Genesis 3:4–6). However, the Devil hid the awful results of that sin. "Wherefore, as by one man sin entered into the world, and death by sin" (Romans 5:12).

The strategy of the pastor's daughter to beat me at Rock, Scissors, Paper was cute to watch, but there's nothing cute whatsoever about the Devil's strategy to tempt us, for as James 1:15 tells us, "Sin, when it is finished, bringeth forth death." Beware of playing "games" with the Devil, because you never know what he has up his sleeve.

THE GIRL WHO MADE ME ANGRY

I took the day off today, and the weather was nice, so in the afternoon I took my daughter to the park. It's quite a large park with several interesting sliding boards. One of them is in the shape of an octopus, so the legs of the octopus are the sliding boards. My daughter was not quite big enough to make it to the top of the sliding board by herself, so I took her hand and helped her. As she stood at the top of the slide, I noticed another girl about the same age trying to climb the ladder, so I took my eyes off of my daughter for just a couple of seconds and helped the other girl to the top.

During those few seconds, an older girl shoved my daughter out of the way and went down the slide. My daughter fell to the ground, and when I turned around, she was lying flat on her back. As I held my crying daughter, my heart was filled with anger. I couldn't imagine that any child could be so mean as to push my daughter off the slide while I was helping another child. It's a good thing the older girl ran away, because if I could have gotten my hands on her, I'm afraid of what I might have done.

My anger remained with me for several hours. I began to complain to God. "My daughter was having so much fun. Why did this have to happen, especially since I was trying to help another child?" Immediately, the Lord spoke to my heart and said, "The same thing happened to me. I was trying to help mankind and they crucified my child."

I felt a sense of shame and became acutely aware of my lack of spiritual growth. My heart was filled with anger toward the girl who had pushed my daughter off of the slide, but God's heart was filled with love toward those who crucified His Son. To be the kind of people God desires us to be, our hearts must become hearts full of love, hearts that can forgive others. "And be ye kind one to another, tenderhearted, forgiving one another, even as God for Christ's sake hath forgiven you" (Ephesians 4:32).

Ken Board

WHEN TWO RINGS BECAME ONE

I always become nervous when I have to conduct a wedding, for there has been some sort of "happening" at almost every wedding I have ever conducted. Because of an incident that took place during my daughter's wedding, I especially become nervous about the rings.

My daughter's wedding was proceeding smoothly until the time came for the bridegroom to take the ring from the small pillow held by the ring boy. When he pulled the ribbon holding the ring in place, the ribbon ended up in a knot that he couldn't untie.

After a while, the best man tried his hand at untying the knot, and when he too couldn't untie it, the bride joined the group and for what seemed like several minutes, the three of them stood in a circle around the small pillow. Finally, the pastor conducting the wedding pulled a small knife out of his pocket and cut the ribbon. Because this incident is imbedded in my memory, I always become tense when it is time for the ring exchange.

I had gone to Okinawa to conduct the wedding of the son of a pastor friend and I was greatly relieved when I was able to remove both rings quickly. It was in the next instant that the "happening" occurred. When I took both rings into my hand, the bride's ring became stuck inside the bridegroom's ring. While trying to think of something to say, I hid my hands behind the pulpit and kept working with the rings until I was able to separate them. It took only a few seconds, but it seemed like a few minutes to me.

Whenever I remember that incident, a passage in the second chapter of Genesis comes to mind. "And the rib, which the Lord God had taken from man, made he a woman, and brought her unto the man. And Adam said, This is now bone of my bones, and flesh of my flesh: she shall be called Woman, because she was taken out of Man. Therefore shall a man leave his father and mother, and shall cleave unto his wife, and they shall be one flesh" (verses 22–24).

Although I was able to separate two rings that had been joined together, in Matthew 19:6 the Lord Jesus gave us this command concerning the bride and bridegroom who are joined together: "What therefore God hath joined together, let not man put asunder."

I DON'T WANT TO GO
TO WAKAMIYA

When I go to the Kanda church, usually I get on the City Expressway at Kurosaki and go all the way to Nagano. From there I take route 10 to the church. However, one Sunday I decided to go from the Kurosaki entrance to Yahata and get on the Kyushu Expressway. As I approached the Yahata exit, I was thinking about something and missed the road to Kanda. I had no choice but to head in the opposite direction, so, griping all the way, I drove to Wakamiya (about eight miles), got off the expressway, got right back on, and drove to church.

The next Sunday I was watching carefully as I approached the Yahata exit, but the only road I could see was a narrow road leading off to the left. As I wondered, "Is that narrow road the road that goes to the church?" I drove right past the road, so again I had to drive all the way to Wakamiya, get off, get right back on, and head toward the church.

The next Sunday, being fully confident that the narrow road was the road I should take, I was able to go to church without having to go in the opposite direction all the way to Wakamiya. I didn't want to go to Wakamiya even once, but I ended up going that far twice.

Occasionally, Christians have the same experience in their spiritual life. We want to obey the teachings of the Bible and walk the right road, but every once in a while we end up going in the wrong direction. Even the apostle Paul experienced this. In the seventh chapter of Romans he wrote, "For what I would do, that do I not; but what I hate, that I do. For the good that I would I do not: but the evil which I would not, that I do. O wretched man that I am! Who shall deliver me from the body of this death? I thank God through Jesus Christ our Lord" (verses 15, 19, 24–25).

Hallelujah! Through the power of the Lord Jesus who lives in every Christian, it is possible to proceed in the direction that is pleasing to the Lord.

Ken Board

SHARING GUM WITH TATSURO

While my wife was shopping, my daughter and I went to the candy store and bought some gum. On her gum was a picture of a rabbit and on my gum was a picture of a bear. In the car on the way home my daughter asked suddenly, "In the Bible it says that we should share with other people, doesn't it?"

When I heard her question, I was extremely happy. I thought, "My daughter is only five years old, but she remembered the teaching of the Bible and wants to obey it."

When I replied, "Yes, that's right," she said, "Then let's share the gum with Tatsuro." (Tatsuro is a small boy that lives in the same neighborhood.)

I was overjoyed at my daughter's willingness to share with her friend, but my joy disappeared when she said, "Daddy, you share your gum with Tatsuro."

I was proud of my daughter's desire to follow the Bible, but I wasn't too pleased with her childish interpretation of Scripture. One of the prominent characteristics of Christians who have not matured spiritually is a self-centered interpretation of the Bible. Because they have not grown sufficiently in faith and in spiritual discernment, they have a tendency to interpret the Bible to match their own preconceived ideas and prejudices.

"For every one that useth milk is unskillful in the word of righteousness: for he is a babe" (Hebrews 5:13). The Christian who has knowledge of the Word of God but uses it to promote his own opinions and feelings resembles a five-year-old child who believes in sharing as long it is not her own gum.

TWO PACKS OF TISSUE

I was at the Fukuoka airport waiting for my flight to Osaka when I reached in my pocket for my handkerchief, but I had picked up my suit at the cleaners just the day before and had forgotten to put a handkerchief in the pocket. I thought, "Great. I'm going to be in Osaka for three days without a handkerchief."

I entered a store to buy a gift for the pastor who had invited me to preach. (In Japan it is a custom to take a gift when you visit someone.) When the store person handed me my receipt, she said, "There's a lottery today, so take this receipt to the store next door." (The Japanese conduct a lottery by having you turn a wheel that has small balls of various colors inside it. The color of the ball determines your prize.)

When I handed my receipt to the young man conducting the drawing, he told me to turn the wheel once. When I did, a black ball fell out. The young man said, "You've won a prize," and handed me a ballpoint pen. As I turned to leave, he said, "Here, take some tissue too," and handed me two small packs of tissue, which are usually set aside for people who do not win anything.

I like ballpoint pens, so I was happy, but I was rejoicing even more for the tissue. Thanking the Lord for the tissue, I headed for the departure lobby.

Of course, there are people who will say, "Your receiving the tissue didn't have anything to do with God. You were just lucky." You could never make me believe that.

According to the Bible, our God is a God who can do "big" miracles, but He is also a God who can do "small" miracles in the daily lives of the people who trust in Him. In Luke 12:6–7 the Lord Jesus said, "Are not five sparrows sold for two farthings, and not one of them is forgotten before God? But even the very hairs of your head are numbered. Fear not therefore: ye are of more value than many sparrows."

If God is concerned with the small sparrow and the number of hairs on my head, surely He is able to supply two packs of tissue to one of His servants who forgot his handkerchief. When we understand this, we should be able to live our Christian life with a heart that is overflowing with courage and hope.

Ken Board

WHEN APRIL'S HOPE TURNS TO OCTOBER'S DESPAIR

It was the beginning of April and my hopes for a championship season for my favorite baseball team were high. "This year," I thought, "this year we'll win the World Series." Of course, millions of other fans embraced the same hope. For example, the fans of the team that barely missed the championship last year were abounding with excitement and expectation of a championship. Even the fans of the team that finished in last place last year or the fans of teams that haven't won a championship in many years grasped the small hope that "this may be the year."

I grew up in Roanoke, Virginia, and all the Brooklyn Dodger games were broadcast in my town, so I have been a lifelong Dodger fan. Last year the Dodgers won their division championship but lost in the playoffs, so this year I had good reason to hope for a championship.

That was April. Now it is October and my hope has turned to despair. My beloved Dodgers finished the season in fifth place.

It seems that many of our hopes in this world end in despair. Of course, there are times when our hopes are fulfilled, but it seems like the times when they turn to despair are many times more plenteous. Therefore, as a Christian, I rejoice in the fact that the hopes we have placed in the Word of God will never end in despair. Because we have assurance of this truth, we can "rejoice in hope" (Romans 12:12). Also, according to Romans 15:13, the God of hope fills us with all joy and peace in believing, that we may abound in hope.

It's always April in the heart of the Christian who has put his hope in the promises of God, and when October rolls around, that hope will turn into joy.

The Amusings of a Missionary

IT FLEW OUT OF
THE FIRE TRUCK WINDOW

We were on our way home from the Wednesday evening service. On the way, we ended up behind a fire truck. Suddenly, something flew out the window of the truck. It was a cigarette. Under normal circumstances I wouldn't have given it a second thought, but the cigarette was still burning!

I thought, "No way! There's no way that someone riding in a fire truck would throw a burning cigarette out of the window." I was rather tired, so I thought perhaps I was seeing things, but I could tell from the shocked look on the faces of everyone else in the car that the burning cigarette was real.

Fire trucks often drive around with loudspeakers blaring, "Be on guard against fires," but now a burning cigarette, one of the main causes of fires, had been thrown from the window of one of those fire trucks. It was unreal.

If our words and actions do not match, the faith we confess with our mouth may seem unreal to the people with whom we associate. We may have the ability to give a splendid testimony at church, but if we go places where a Christian should not go or speak words that a Christian should not speak, our splendid testimony will seem like nothing more than a skillful lie to the people who watch our actions.

In 1 John 2:3–4 the Bible teaches, "And hereby we do know that we know him, if we keep his commandments. He that saith, I know him, and keepeth not his commandments, is a liar, and the truth is not in him."

Ken Board

A DAY IN MY PAJAMAS

Every morning I take a shower and comb my hair before breakfast. When I eat breakfast, I still have on my pajamas, but I change clothes right after breakfast.

One day when I woke up, I thought, "All my work today is desk work here at the house. I have no plans to go out, and I don't expect anyone to come, so I'll just spend the day in my pajamas." I took a shower, but I put my pajamas back on and didn't even comb my hair.

I was working on Sunday's message when the doorbell rang. I reluctantly went to the door. One of the neighborhood ladies stood at the door. She said, "It's your turn to clean up after the garbage next week." (In Japan, instead of putting the garbage in front of each house, everyone in the block has to take it to the same place. Then, after the garbage truck comes, someone has to go and clean that place.)

Until now, whenever that lady had come to tell me about the garbage, she had always left quickly, but because she knows I am working at a church, this day she suddenly started asking my advice about a family problem. Still wearing my pajamas and with my hair in a mess, I stood in the doorway for about thirty minutes and talked with her.

I was quite embarrassed to open the door to my neighbor when I still had on my pajamas and my hair was a mess, but I can think of something much more embarrassing. In 2 Corinthians 5:10 it is written, "For we must all appear before the judgment seat of Christ; that every one may receive the things done in his body, according to that he hath done, whether it be good or bad." Therefore, let us live a life that is pleasing to the Lord so there will be no need to be embarrassed when we stand before Him. While it is unsettling to have to stand at the door and talk with a neighbor lady for thirty minutes in my pajamas with my hair disheveled, it would be much more unsettling to have to stand before the Lord with a disheveled heart.

"And now, little children, abide in him; that, when he shall appear, we may have confidence, and not be ashamed before him at his coming" (1 John 2:28).

LOOK OUT! SNAKE ON THE LOOSE!

My family and I decided to take a vacation in Miyazaki on the southeastern shore of the island of Kyushu. When we checked into our hotel, it was still early, so we decided to visit a nearby zoo. As we entered the zoo, we had to climb a small hill. As we neared the top of the hill, we saw a zoo employee pounding the ground with a shovel.

When we reached the top of the hill, we saw the cause of all the commotion. There was a long silver-colored snake on the ground, and the zoo employee was trying to kill it with the shovel; however, the snake quickly slithered out of danger into some brush. Naturally, I expected the zoo employee to pursue the snake until he could catch it and kill it, but he threw the shovel into his wheelbarrow and, glancing from side to side, quickly left the area.

I couldn't believe it. I thought, "What an irresponsible fellow you are!" It was quite a nice zoo, but my family and I didn't enjoy it because the whole time we were there we kept wondering, "Where's the snake? Where's the snake?" We were careful to avoid any areas where we thought the snake might be hiding.

The Bible calls the Devil a "that old serpent which deceiveth the whole world" (Revelation 12:9). According to 1 Peter 5:8, the Devil "walketh about, seeking whom he may devour."

It could be that there is a "snake" on the loose in some of the places we like to gather. Therefore, let us pay heed to Paul's admonition in Ephesians 5:15 to "walk circumspectly" and avoid places where we might be tempted to participate in actions that are dangerous to our Christian life.

Ken Board

"WHERE DID YOU PUT THE MEASURING CUP?"

Each night after supper my wife and I would do the dishes together. She would wash the dishes and I would dry them and put them into the cabinet. I knew where most of the dishes were supposed to go, but occasionally there would be something that I did not know where to put, so I would just put it in any old place where it would fit. As a result, my wife would not be able to find the things she needed to prepare the meal.

The other day my wife asked me, "Where did you put the measuring cup?"

When I answered, "I put it where I always put it," she replied, "No, it's not there. Where did you put it?"

I repeated, "I put it where I always put it," but my wife didn't believe me.

A few minutes later she yelled, "I found the measuring cup. It was still inside the bag of flour where I had left it."

I wanted to say, "See there. You thought it was my fault, but you were the one who misplaced the cup," but I've been married long enough to know when to speak up and when to be silent, so I decided to keep quiet.

According to the Bible, from the time of Adam and Eve, there has been a tendency in man to make his own sins and mistakes the fault of someone else. When Adam sinned and was confronted by the Lord, he replied, "The woman whom thou gavest to be with me, she . . ." (Genesis 3:12)

When God said to the woman, "What is this that thou hast done?" she defended herself by saying, "The serpent . . ." (3:13)

This tendency in man to blame others for his sins and mistakes continues to this day. However, according to the Bible, when we sin, the person who will receive the mercy of God is the person who will humble himself before God and admit his sins and take responsibility for them.

IT WAS JUST A LITTLE BIT!

I emptied the can of kerosene when I filled up the kerosene stove, but it wasn't completely empty. There was still just a little bit of kerosene left in the can. No matter how hard I tried, I couldn't empty the can completely. When I shook the can, I could hear that little bit of kerosene sloshing around the bottom of the can. It was just a little bit, so when I put the lid on the kerosene can, I didn't close it tightly.

Later, I put the can in the car and went to buy some more kerosene. On the way, the can turned over and the lid came off and that little bit of kerosene spilled in the car. You would not believe how much of a smell came from that little bit of kerosene! I tried scrubbing the spot where that little bit of kerosene had spilled. I tried air freshener. Nothing worked. It was just a little bit, but the car smelled like kerosene for about a week.

In the same way, as we try to live a life that is pleasing to the Lord, usually the sins that trouble us are not the so-called "big" sins. Normally, Christians do not commit the "big" sins like idolatry, murder, and theft, but we are often troubled by the so-called "little" sins. In Song of Solomon 2:15 the Bible uses the expression "the little foxes that spoil the grapes." There were no large holes in the wall around Solomon's vineyard, so the big foxes could not enter, but the little foxes found the small holes and came in and ate the grapes. Let's be careful of the so-called "little" sins. Let's be on guard against sins like unkindness, impatience, selfishness, and a critical attitude. There is a proverb that says, "Men stumble over pebbles, not mountains."

Ken Board

THE CAT THAT SOUNDED LIKE A BIRD AND THE BIRD THAT SOUNDED LIKE A CAT

I was studying at my desk when I heard a strange sound. It sounded like one of the birds that often come and sit on top of the shed in our yard. This sound was closer than that, however, so I got up, looked around, and saw our cat sitting at the window calling to the birds on top of the shed. The sound the cat was making sounded exactly like the sound the birds make. I think our cat was trying to trick one of the birds into flying over to the window.

A couple of months later when I was out shopping with my family, I saw a bird sitting in a cage in front of a restaurant. There are birds that will repeat words, so I stopped and said, "Hello," to the bird. The bird didn't answer. I tried, "Good morning," but the bird was silent. Just then the owner of the bird came out of the restaurant, saw me trying to get the bird to talk, and explained, "This bird can't speak any words, but it can meow like a cat." I stood there for a while, and all of a sudden the bird said, "Meooow." The bird sounded identical to our cat!

Perhaps you have never seen a cat that sounded like a bird and a bird that sounded like a cat, but I did once in my life. Our cat and that bird remind me of false teachers who are calling Christians to doctrines that are not biblical. These false teachers delight in using words like "love" and "peace" and quoting Bible passages to lure Christians away from their churches and the fundamental teachings of the Bible.

The Lord Jesus Christ Himself warned us about these false teachers: "Beware of false prophets, which come to you in sheep's clothing, but inwardly they are ravening wolves" (Matthew 7:15). Please allow me to explain this passage with words based on my own experience. "Beware of false prophets who resemble cats that sound like birds and birds that sound like cats."

TAP, TAP, TAP

This summer I had my yard work done by an organization called Silver, a group of retired people who do odd jobs. Usually, one lady and one man come and work in the yard about half a day. The man is not always the same person, but it's always the same lady. She's a very interesting lady. The first time she came to my home, she came to the front door, but ever since that first time, she always goes to the rear of the house and taps on the window.

The first time she did that, I was working at my desk. Suddenly, I heard "Tap, tap, tap." Wondering what in the world the noise was, I looked around but saw nothing unusual. Again I heard "Tap, tap, tap," so I went to the window and opened the curtain. That lady was standing in my yard tapping on my window. Since then I have been surprised several times by her sudden "tap, tap, tap." One day I was lying in bed with my pajamas on, and she came to my bedroom window and tapped on it.

I have no idea when she will come again, but now when I hear "Tap, tap, tap," I immediately yell, "Okay," and go to the window.

She reminds me of the Lord. We don't know when and where the Lord will tap on our heart, but we should constantly be in a state of mind that can hear the Lord's tap any time and any place.

One night a young man named Samuel was sleeping. Suddenly, God called Samuel. In fact, he called Samuel three times, but Samuel couldn't determine who it was that was calling him. Finally, when God called him the fourth time, Samuel followed the instructions of Eli and replied, "Speak, Lord, for thy servant heareth" (1 Samuel 3:10).

When we realize that the Lord is tapping on our heart, let's be quick to reply, "Speak, Lord, for thy servant heareth."

Ken Board

TRAFFIC JAMS AND FOGGY ROADS

Should we take Route 10 or the Kyushu Expressway? This was the problem being pondered by the church people who had gathered that morning, especially the four drivers. We considered taking the expressway, but after a time of prayer we felt led to proceed with our plan to take Route 10 to the summer camp in Oita. It was *Obon*, a time when many Japanese return home, so we knew that no matter which road we took, it would be crowded.

Sure enough, between Yukuhashi and Usa we ran into a traffic jam. Immediately, I thought, "We made the wrong choice. We should have taken the expressway." But then I turned on the radio and found out that there was a sixty-mile traffic jam on the expressway! If we had gone that way, we would have missed all of the activities and services of the first day of camp. As it was, the trip that normally takes three and one-half hours took two hours longer, but we arrived in time for supper and the evening service. We thanked the Lord for His guidance.

On the way home there was no traffic jam, but near Beppu we ran into a dense fog. The fog was so thick that I could see none of the road signs or even the white line in the middle of the road. I am quite fearful of driving in foggy weather, so I was growing more and more tense by the moment, but I was helped by two things.

First of all, the driver of the car in front of me had his lights on, so I followed close behind him until he pulled into a rest area. Also, two of the church members were riding with me, one in the passenger seat and one in the backseat. The two of them opened the windows, one on the left and one on the right, and helped me stay in my lane, so we made it home safely.

When the roads of life become foggy and we lose sight of the path we ought to walk, help comes from two sources. First, there is the light of the Word of God. "Thy word is a lamp unto my feet, and a light unto my path" (Psalm 119:105). Also, there are the prayers of our brothers and sisters in Christ. In his Second Epistle to the Corinthians, Paul wrote, "Ye also helping together by prayer for us" (1:11).

When it seems that we about to lose our way, let's turn to the Word of God for light and to our friends for helpful prayers.

COMEDY AT THE TOLLGATE

On the way to Hiraodai to have a picnic with the members of another church, there was a scene that resembled a TV comedy. My van went first and one of the church ladies followed in her car. When we arrived at the Kyushu Expressway tollgate, the comedy began. The lady was used to the Kitakyushu City Expressway, where you pay before you enter the road, but she rarely uses the Kyushu Expressway, where you take a toll ticket and pay when you exit the road. She drove through the tollgate without taking a ticket and then realized her mistake and sent another lady running back to ask for one.

I was watching this and laughed, but in the next moment it was my turn to come on stage. As I neared the tollgate, I realized that I did not have my ETC (Electronic Toll Collection) card ready. As I entered the tollgate I desperately searched for the card and inserted it just as I entered the gate, but I was a little too late. The gentleman in charge of the tollgate instructed me to back up and go through the regular gate. I tried to explain that I had my card, but again he instructed me to back up and go through the regular gate. After getting the car and the bus behind me to back up, I went through the regular gate and took a toll ticket. I had intended to prepare the ETC card ahead of time, but suddenly there I was entering the gate with no card.

This incident resembles the occasions when we intend to do some sort of work for the Lord, but end up being too late. For example, we keep thinking, "Some day I am going to tell that man about Christ," and then one day we receive word that he has passed away. A Christian life composed of things we intend to do some day is not a good Christian life. I wanted to go through the ETC gate, but when I couldn't, thankfully I was able to back up and go through another gate. However, in the Christian life, when we intend to do some work for the Lord and are too late, we may not be able to return to the place where we lost the opportunity.

After we arrived at Hiraodai, the church ladies and I had a good laugh, but when something like this takes place in our Christian life, it is not a comedy. It is a tragedy. "See then that ye walk circumspectly, not as fools, but as wise, Redeeming the time . . ." (Ephesians 5:15–16).

Ken Board

THE MELTED BASKET

Both my wife and I told our daughter over and over again, "Don't leave things, especially plastic things, on top of the kerosene heater. They will melt." In spite of all of our repeated warnings, one day when I was working at my desk, I was suddenly interrupted by screams coming out of the next room. I jumped up and ran into the room and saw a plastic basket sitting on top of the stove. Half of it had already melted and dripped down into the stove. I turned the stove off as quickly as I could, but the basket was ruined.

In Numbers 32:23 the Bible warns us, "Be sure your sin will find you out." When we have knowledge of the commandments of the Lord but choose to ignore them, we will have to suffer the consequences of our action. Because our daughter ignored our words of caution, she ended up losing her favorite basket that she took with her when she went shopping.

In addition, our acts of disobedience or carelessness cause problems for other people too. It took my wife over an hour and a half to clean the stove.

Even though we may repent later and receive the forgiveness of the Lord, we may not be able to avoid the results of our actions. Our daughter said, "Daddy, Mama, I'm sorry," but her words could not return her favorite basket or her mother's valuable time.

Therefore, because we know that "our sins will find us out," let us pay heed to the commandments of the Lord. If we don't, we may lose something much more valuable than a plastic basket.

TOO MUCH CHANGE

As soon as our daughter received her 500 yen (about $5) allowance from her mother, she asked me to take her to the bookstore. She chose a book that cost 440 yen, paid for it, received her change, and we stepped outside the store. She counted her change and said, "Daddy, the change is wrong." I took the change from her and counted it. It should have been 60 yen, but it was 160 yen. Immediately, we went back into the store and returned 100 yen to the clerk.

I was so proud of my daughter. One hundred yen is a lot of money to a small child. She could have kept the extra hundred yen a secret and bought herself some ice cream, but she chose to do the right thing. I was so happy that I gave her an extra hundred yen.

Every day the child of God must judge between right and wrong many times. Of course, we always do the right thing when someone is watching, but what about when we are by ourselves?

According to Psalm 44:21, God knows the secrets of the heart. Also, in Psalm 90:8 it is written, "Thou hast set our iniquities before thee, our secret sins in the light of our countenance." Therefore, the person who is trying to hide his sins and keep them a secret should realize the folly of his action and pray the prayer written in Psalm 19:12: "Cleanse me from secret faults."

If there is a hundred yen in our pocket that shouldn't be there, let's do the right thing as quickly as possible. The prayer that David prayed in Psalm 139:23–24 is a prayer that all Christians should pray regularly: "Search me, O God, and know my heart: try me, and know my thoughts. And see if there be any wicked way in me, and lead me in the way everlasting."

Ken Board

DON'T THROW THE CUSHIONS!

My son and I were watching sumo on television. The second highest rank in sumo is called "Champion" and the highest rank is called "Grand Champion." At the time there were two Champions and four Grand Champions. Both Champions and the first three Grand Champions proceeded to lose, one after another.

When the last Grand Champion stepped up for his match, I told my son, "If he loses too, the fans will throw their cushions today." Although there are regular seats too, most people sit on cushions in small boxes just barely wide enough for four people. Always before the final match, there will be an announcement: "Please don't throw the cushions." However, if the Grand Champion is upset in the final match, the fans usually ignore the announcement and display their excitement by throwing their cushions. Already today, two Champions and three Grand Champions had been upset, so I knew that the cushions were going to fly if the fourth Grand Champion lost too.

If sumo fans become excited enough to throw cushions, how much more excited should Christians become when someone receives Christ as his personal Savior. After all, isn't the salvation of a soul many times more wonderful than the upset of a Grand Champion? Isn't the greatest thrill of the Christian life the thrill of leading another person to Christ?

Recently, a young lady was saved at our church. We had been praying for her salvation for several weeks. When she confessed her sins to God and received the Lord Jesus Christ as her personal Savior, I was looking for some cushions to throw. In fact, I have even thought about getting rid of the church chairs and have everyone sit on cushions so we can throw them every time someone gets saved.

Of course, I am joking, but we ought to be filled with excitement whenever a precious soul comes to Christ. "Likewise, I say unto you, there is joy in the presence of the angels of God over one sinner that repenteth" (Luke 15:10).

THERE WAS ONE MORE SWITCH

I arrived in the Chiba area about three o'clock in the afternoon and decided to take a shower before that evening's special service in which I was scheduled to speak. The pastor took me into the shower room and explained in detail what I needed to do to turn on the hot water. Thinking I had it all figured out, I began my shower, but even though I did exactly as the pastor had explained, there was no hot water. I turned on the left faucet and let the water run for a while, but it didn't get warm at all. I turned that faucet off and turned on the right faucet and let the water run for a while, but the result was the same.

According to the pastor's explanation, if I turned the handle on the shower to the right, there would be hot water. I turned it to the right, to the left, and then back to the right again, but only cold water came out. Finally, I just gave up and took a cold shower. It was quite chilly but it was refreshing.

Later I found out that there was one more switch in the kitchen that controlled the hot water, and unless that switch was turned on, a person could stand in the shower and turn handles and faucets all day long to no avail. Until someone turned on that switch, there would be no hot water.

Unless we are filled with the power of the Holy Spirit, our evangelistic efforts will resemble a cold shower. We may mimic the methods of a church where multitudes are gathering, or we may follow in detail the methods explained in the book of a famous author, but unless the leaders and members of the church are filled with the power of the Holy Spirit, our evangelism will not be fruitful evangelism.

In Romans 15:13 Paul wrote, "Now the God of hope fill you with all joy and peace in believing, that ye may abound in hope, through the power of the Holy Ghost," and then in verse 19 he added, "Through mighty signs and wonders, by the power of the Spirit of God, I have fully preached the gospel of Christ."

"By the power of the Spirit of God"—that's the "switch" that turns on the "hot water" of God's blessing on our evangelism.

Ken Board

TOASTED BREAD
AND TOASTED FINGERS

The hotel in Kaohsiung provided all guests an all-you-can-eat breakfast, so I headed for the restaurant with great anticipation only to discover that more than half of the "delicacies" resembled food that might have come from the prodigal son's hog pen. I'm certain the Oriental guests enjoyed the food, but most of it looked gross to me. However, I saw some delicious-looking bread and what I assumed was a microwave oven, so I put two pieces of bread on a plate and placed the plate into the microwave.

Immediately, the plate and bread began moving toward the back of the oven. I was afraid the plate would fall out of the back of the oven and break, so I reached in and pulled the plate toward the front. The plate was hot, so I burned my fingers, and while I was blowing on my fingers, the plate slowly moved toward the back of the oven again. I burned my fingers again when I reached into the oven and pulled out the plate.

Thinking, "What a weird microwave oven," I decided to watch the man who had been waiting behind me. He took two pieces of bread and placed only the bread into the oven. When it reached the back of the oven, the hot bread fell onto a tray beneath the oven, and the man used some tongs to pick up the bread and place it on his plate. That's when I realized that it wasn't a microwave oven. It was a toaster oven. Because the man had shown me the right way of using the oven, the next morning I was able to enjoy some delicious hot bread without burning my fingers.

According to Proverbs 14:12, "There is a way which seemeth right unto a man, but the end thereof are the ways of death." Just as I needed someone to show me the right way to use the oven, man needs someone to show him the right path to walk.

Verse 21 of 1 Peter chapter 2 identifies that person for us. "Christ suffered for us, leaving us an example, that ye should follow his steps." And then, in verse 24, the Bible says, "Who his own self bare our sins in his own body on the tree, that we, being dead to sins, should live unto righteousness."

Every person who is seeking the right way should turn his eyes to the holy example of the Savior and follow His steps.

THE BOX OF DONUTS

Since it is a custom in Japan to take a gift when you visit someone, last month when we went to a church in Kagoshima Prefecture, the other missionary and I both took a gift to the church. Since the church is way out in the country, he thought, "There's probably not a donut shop on the island," so he took a box of donuts. I took some special cakes that are made in my area, and because I know that the pastor and his wife love *mentai* (fish eggs), I took some *mentai* too.

When we arrived at the church, both of us sat our gifts on the floor. While he went out for a while with his family, the pastor and I went into another room and enjoyed a time of fellowship. After everyone returned to the church, we had supper there, and then the pastor's wife announced, "Tonight's dessert is donuts." When she picked up the box of donuts that had been sitting on the floor for about four hours and opened it, the box was full of ants. During the time we were having our time of fellowship and eating supper, the ants had carried away about half of the donuts.

When the pastor's wife told us what had happened, immediately I thought of two Bible passages. "Go to the ant, thou sluggard; consider her ways, and be wise: Which having no guide, overseer, or ruler, Provideth her meat in the summer, and gathereth her food in the harvest" (Proverbs 6:6–8). "The ants are a people not strong, yet they prepare their meat in the summer" (Proverbs 30:25).

We can learn two lessons from the ants that carried away the donuts. First, we can learn the importance of preparation. The person who desires to do the work of God should make sufficient preparation with a specific goal in mind.

The second lesson we learn is the importance of cooperation. One ant could not have carried away even one donut, but when they combined their power, they were able to carry away nearly half of the donuts.

One of the secrets of the growth of the church in Jerusalem recorded in the book of Acts was cooperation. "And the multitude of them that believed were of one heart and of one soul" (Acts 4:32). We too can look forward to the growth of our church when the members are of one heart and one soul.

Ken Board

FROM ZERO TO FIFTY-ONE

One day my family had lunch at a local restaurant. When I paid the bill, I was handed three soft-drink coupons, so the next time we ate at that restaurant, each one of us had a drink for only fifty cents each. When I paid the bill, I was given several more drink coupons.

Each time, the coupons I received were more than the coupons that I used, so the coupons began to increase. For example, the other day I took my wife, my daughter, and another pastor out to eat. I gave the waiter four coupons and received six or seven more when I paid the bill. When I counted the coupons in the glove compartment of my car, there were twenty-three of them. But that's not all. My wife had twenty-eight more in her purse. In a period of four to five years, the number of those drink coupons had increased from zero to fifty-one.

The blessings of the Christian life are similar to those coupons. In Luke 6:38 the Lord Jesus said, "Give, and it shall be given unto you; good measure, pressed down, and shaken together, and running over, shall men give into your bosom." Of course, our motive in serving the Lord is not to receive blessings, but it is a fact that blessings will be given to those who give. For example, it may require some sort of sacrifice to give our time to the Lord to serve Him at church, but the blessings we receive from the Lord will far surpass that sacrifice.

Let's test this "give and it shall be given unto you" principle and see if it really works. In 2 Corinthians 9:8 the Bible says, "And God is able to make all grace abound toward you; that ye, always having all sufficiency in all things, may abound to every good work." Let's believe the Word of God and trust that the Lord will make the life of the person who has a giving heart a life that is overflowing with "blessing coupons."

THE FIFTH BAG

I returned from the grocery store and set the grocery bags on the kitchen table. I counted the bags. There were five of them, but there were supposed be only four.

Wondering, "What's in the extra bag?" I opened them one by one and looked at the contents. Four of them were filled with groceries, but the fifth one was filled with empty milk cartons. (In Japan we are not allowed to throw empty milk cartons in the garbage. Instead, after we have collected a few, we take them back to the grocery store and leave them in a recycling center.) Intending to take my empty milk cartons to the recycling center, I had put them into a grocery bag and carried them from my house to the grocery store. However, after I arrived at the store, I forgot all about the milk cartons and ended up carrying them back to my house with my groceries.

Just as there are both things you should get rid of and things you should purchase at a Japanese grocery store, in the Christian's life there are things he should get rid of and things he should add. In 2 Peter 1:5–7 we are told to "add to your faith virtue; and to virtue knowledge; and to knowledge temperance; and to temperance patience; and to patience godliness; and to godliness brotherly kindness; and to brotherly kindness charity."

In order to grow spiritually, there are also things that we should throw away. According to 1 Peter 2:1 we are to "lay aside all malice, and all guile, and hypocrisies, and envies, and all evil speaking."

When we go before the Lord, let's receive the virtues that are necessary to become a person whom God can use. At the same time, we must not forget to get rid of the vices in our life.

Ken Board

THAT AWFUL SOUND

It was about seven o'clock in the morning. If I didn't hurry to the hospital and put my name on the list, I would have to wait quite a while when I went to get my medicine later. (There is no appointment system at most hospitals and clinics in Japan.) I jumped into my car and hurriedly backed out of my parking space. In the next instant I heard that awful sound. It is a sound that I have heard many times before, namely the sound of my fender scraping the wall.

The parking space at my home is narrow and there are concrete walls on both sides. I have scraped those walls with my car many times, but the scraping sound was especially unpleasant this time, for I had purchased the car just sixteen days earlier. It was a used car, but it didn't have a scratch on it, so when I heard that awful sound, I felt like crying.

Later I took the car to several repair shops for estimates and the cheapest one was $400. If I could get back all the money that I have paid over the years to repair damages caused by scraping the walls of my parking place, I would probably be a wealthy man.

Every time I scrape the walls with my car, the cause is always the same. I am in too much of a hurry. If I took the time to watch both sides of the car when I entered or exited my parking space, I probably would never scrape the wall.

On many occasions the cause of the scars on our heart is the same cause. In other words, the more we hurry, the more likely we are to be careless. In Proverbs 21:5 the Bible says, "The thoughts of the diligent tend only to plenteousness; but of everyone that is hasty only to want."

When we hear a report that causes us concern, our first tendency may be to rush around in all directions. The image of a chicken that has just lost its head portrays well the image of many people who have just experienced an unhappy event. However, the person who is trusting in the Lord doesn't need to react to the events of life in that manner.

"Wait on the Lord: be of good courage, and he shall strengthen thine heart: wait, I say, on the Lord" (Psalm 27:14).

"GRAB BAG" DEVOTIONS

Right now our son is using an unusual method to choose the Bible passage for his daily devotions. He reaches his hand into a bag and pulls out a page of the Bible. Whatever portion of the Bible happens to be on that page is his passage for his devotions.

This all came about as a result of the actions of a dog that our son was keeping for his friend. One morning when our son finished his devotions, instead of returning his Bible to the bookcase, he left it on his desk. While he was at work, the dog got hold of the Bible and tore it apart and scattered it all over the room. When our son came home from work, he scooped up the pages of his Bible and stuffed them into a bag. When our son related this incident to us on the phone, my wife named his devotions "Grab Bag" devotions. I honestly can't recommend this method to any Christians, but I was happy about one thing. The fact that my son was having devotions every morning gave me great joy.

There are a lot of opinions concerning the method, time, and place for having devotions, but isn't the most important thing about devotions not the method or the time or the place but the regularity? I seriously doubt that anyone would want to use the same method as my son's current method, but the important thing is to have fellowship with the Lord daily through prayer and the Bible. Those daily devotions will make the daily walk of the Christian a walk that is pleasing to the Lord.

"Blessed is the man that walketh not in the counsel of the ungodly, nor standeth in the way of sinners, nor sitteth in the seat of the scornful. But his delight is in the law of the Lord; and in his law doth he meditate day and night. And he shall be like a tree planted by the rivers of water, that bringeth forth his fruit in his season; his leaf also shall not wither; and whatsoever he doeth shall prosper" (Psalm 1:1–3).

Ken Board

THE CINDERELLA STRATEGY

Every now and then the police department of Japan comes up with some clever safety campaigns. One of my favorites was: "In small Japan, where do you expect to go driving that fast?" The size of Japan is about the same size as the state of California, and with the modern highway system that we have now, it would probably be possible to drive from the southern island of Kyushu to the northern island of Hokkaido in a couple of days. (No, I have never tried it.)

Probably my favorite slogan of all was one I saw in Okinawa. Here and there were large signs that read: "Cinderella Strategy." It didn't make sense to me until a pastor friend explained it. Many traffic accidents take place after midnight, so it was a campaign to persuade everyone to go home by midnight.

"The Cinderella Strategy"—don't you think this would be a good slogan for church members too? In Psalm 100:2 we find the words, "Serve the Lord with gladness: come before his presence with singing." However, what happens when we stay up past midnight on Saturday evening? Even if we do make it to church, we just barely arrive in time. Furthermore, we are tired and sleepy. We are in no condition at all to serve the Lord "with gladness."

So let's try the "Cinderella Strategy." Let's be at home early on Saturday. Let's turn off the TV and the computer and get plenty of rest so we can joyfully serve the Lord and sing praises to His name. If we want to stay up past midnight on other days of the week, well, that's up to each person to decide, but on Saturday let's put the "Cinderella Strategy" into practice.

"THERE'S A CENTIPEDE ON YOUR NECK!"

I went to visit a church on an island in Kagoshima Prefecture with a pastor friend and a missionary friend and their families. This church is surrounded by woods full of various animals and insects. For example, the night we were there, the pastor's wife heard the cries of a wild boar that had approached the church.

The next morning when we were making preparations to go fishing, I was standing in the parking lot talking with the pastor and his wife. Suddenly, his wife screamed, "There's a centipede on your neck!"

Normally, if there is some sort of insect on my neck, I would brush it off with my hand. If I had done so that day, I probably would have been stung by the centipede. As I leaned my body toward the pastor, he snapped the towel in his hand and knocked the centipede off of my neck and killed it.

On a previous occasion I had seen a rather large centipede inside the church, so when the pastor's wife screamed, "centipede!" the first image that came to my mind was that large centipede. However, when I looked at the dead centipede, I was surprised to see that it was a fairly small centipede only about an inch long. I said to the pastor, "There's no need to get excited over a little centipede like that."

He replied, "Wrong! If that little centipede had stung your neck, your neck would have swollen so large that it would have been necessary to take you to the hospital!"

There is a tendency in man to look at sin the way I looked at that little centipede and divide sins into "little" sins and "big" sins. The so-called "big" sins are sins like murder, theft, and adultery that we absolutely would never commit, while the so-called "little" sins are sins that we don't need to worry about all that much even if we do commit them.

In Colossians 3:5 we are commanded to "mortify" the "big" sins like fornication, uncleanness, and covetousness; however, in verse 8 we are also commanded to "put away" the "little" sins like anger, malice, and filthy communication. There are probably more Christians who turn away from the Lord because of "little" sins than there are Christians who turn away from the Lord because of some "big" sin, so let's watch out for the little centipedes too.

Ken Board

"I'M ALL RIGHT"

When my wife suddenly went home to be with the Lord, my children were quite concerned about me. I have several problems with my health, and I don't know how to cook. Almost every day I would receive a phone call or e-mail message asking, "Daddy, are you all right?"

I visited one of my daughters for several days, and while I was there, she asked me a number of times, "Daddy, are you really all right?"

One morning, I decided to have a bowl of cereal. My daughter entered the kitchen and asked again, "Daddy, are you all right?"

I replied, "I'm fine. Don't worry," and then proceeded to take the orange juice out of the refrigerator and pour it on my cereal. My daughter stood there with an extremely concerned look on her face.

Many of the failures of our Christian life occur when we rely on our own strength and think "I'm all right." In Matthew, chapter 26, the Lord Jesus said to His disciples, "All ye shall be offended because of me this night." Right away Peter replied, "Though all men shall be offended because of thee, yet will I never be offended" (verse 33).

The Lord said unto him, "Verily, I say unto thee, That this night, before the cock crow, thou shalt deny me thrice."

Peter answered, "Though I should die with thee, yet will I not deny thee."

Just as I insisted to my daughter, "I'm all right," Peter insisted to the Lord, "I'm all right."

Christians, when our attitude toward our Christian life becomes "I can do it. I'm all right," we are headed for a fall. In 1 Corinthians 10:12 the Bible says, "Wherefore let him that thinketh he standeth take heed lest he fall." When, instead of trusting in the Lord and relying on His power we become self-confident and exclaim, "I'm all right," we are about five seconds away from pouring orange juice on our cereal.

THE YELLOW, ORANGE, BROWN TRAIN

We were on our way home from shopping when we had to stop at a railroad crossing. My daughter likes to watch trains, so I said to her, "Look! A train is coming. Let's see what color it is." As the train approached, I stated, "It's a yellow train."

My daughter replied, "No, Daddy, it's an orange train."

My wife spoke up and said, "You're both wrong. It's a light brown train."

I'll admit to being somewhat color-blind, but it looked like a yellow train to me. When my daughter looked at the same train, she saw an orange color, and my wife saw a light brown train. I suppose the true color of the train was a mixture of yellow, orange, and light brown, although I have no idea what color a mixture of those three colors would be.

When several people try to decide the color of an object, each person has the right to express his own opinion, but 2 Peter 1:20 teaches us that no one has the right to handle the Bible in the same manner. "No prophecy of scripture is of any private interpretation." Therefore, we when study the Bible, let's remember these three principles.

First, the Bible is the Word of the living God.

Second, it is a mistake to interpret the Bible according to prior experiences and prejudices and opinions that already exist in our heart.

Third, instead of relying on our own mental ability to interpret the Bible, we should rely on the Holy Spirit to teach us the true meaning. If we follow these three principles in our interpretation of the Bible, just as the Lord Jesus promised in John 16:13, the Holy Spirit will guide us into all truth. It is when we look at the Bible through the guidance of the Holy Spirit that we are able to see the true "color" of each verse.

Ken Board

MISTER RAGS

When I went to purchase my new cell phone, the clerk told me that it would take about forty minutes to register the phone, so I went to the food court and had supper and returned to the cell phone counter about fifty minutes later. The clerk said, "It's going to take about five more minutes."

After I had waited a while, the clerk came to where I was sitting and said, "We found the problem. You were registered as Mister *Boro* instead of Mister *Boodo*." (My English name "Board" is pronounced "Boodo" in Japanese.)

I never have been a skillful writer, so when I filled in the original application form, the clerk must have mistaken the last letter in my name for an *o* instead of a *d* and registered my name as "Boro" (Boaro) instead of "Boodo" (Board). She asked, "Do you want us to change the registration?"

I asked, "If you change the name on the registration, will I have to wait any longer?" I was tired of waiting, so when she said, "Yes," I told her to just leave it as it was. I told of all my friends, "When you look for me in the registry of this cell phone company, don't look for *Boodo*. Look for *Boro*."

Actually it wouldn't be a mistake to give the name "Boro" to all people. According to the Bible, all people are "dead in trespasses and sins" (Ephesians 2:1). In Isaiah 64:6 the Bible describes the natural state of all men with these words: "All our righteousness are as filthy rags." The Japanese word for "rags" is *boro*.

It's true. Before we believe in Christ, all of our goodness is nothing more than filthy rags in the sight of God, so I am not the only "Mister Rags." "Rags" is the spiritual last name of all people until they believe in the Lord Jesus and receive Him as their personal Savior. But, wait, there's good news. The same passage (Ephesians 2) that teaches us the sinful condition of the natural man also tells us that the rich mercy and great love of God provided us a way of salvation through Christ Jesus. "For by grace are ye saved through faith" (2:8). The very instant that we believe in Christ, God removes the filthy rags and clothes us in His own righteousness.

I may be listed as "Mister Rags" in the cell phone company's registry, but in God's "Book of Life" I am registered as "Ken Board, sinner saved by grace." Hallelujah!

The Amusings of a Missionary

NICE SHOT!

When we went to visit my son in Kokubu, we went to Matsuyama Park on a mountain overlooking the town. The view was spectacular, and there were several rides, including a roller coaster that is very popular with young people. There was also a miniature golf course.

I have been a big fan of miniature golf since my high school days, so I persuaded everyone to play a round. It was quite a difficult course. On the third hole my wife's ball rolled off of the green into the rough, but her next shot was a beautiful shot that rolled into the hole. We all mimicked the pro golfers we see on TV and shouted, "Nice shot!"

On the eighth hole my wife's ball went off the green into some rough again. It was a much longer shot than the one on the third hole, but again she holed out from the rough. We were all amazed. It wasn't just a "nice shot." It was a miraculous shot.

Well, did my wife win the match that day? No, she didn't. In fact, our son-in-law was the winner. My wife made the two long shots, but she struggled on the other holes while our son-in-law, even though he did not make any spectacular shots, played steady golf on each hole.

The Christian who is able to live a victorious spiritual life is not the Christian who shows up at church just once a month and does something spectacular that amazes everyone. Rather, it is the Christian who attends church every week and serves the Lord faithfully. Christians who are "off and on" in their attendance, service, and giving are not pleasing to the Lord. The Christians who bring joy to the Lord are those who are continually faithful in every aspect of their church life.

"Therefore, my beloved brethren, be ye steadfast, unmoveable, always abounding in the work of the Lord" (1 Corinthians 15:58).

Ken Board

THE ROCK IN MY MAILBOX

If you looked inside my mailbox, you would probably be surprised, for you would see a heavy rock.

When we bought the mailbox, a stand came with it, but there was no suitable place in front of the house to put the stand, so I just sat the mailbox on top of the wall. It was there for several months, but one day I heard that a typhoon was headed our way. I was concerned that the mailbox might be blown away, so I placed a heavy stone inside it. It's not that large a stone, but it's fairly heavy. The typhoon winds were strong, but the mailbox didn't move an inch.

It has now been several years since I placed that stone in the mailbox. In that time several typhoons have passed through this area, but the mailbox supported by the stone is still on the wall in front of our house.

Just as there was a storm with the power to damage our mailbox, there are storms with the power to damage our lives. Sooner or later all people will experience storms such as sickness, loss of employment, and the death of a loved one. However, when the storms come, if we are standing on the Rock, the Lord Jesus Christ, there will be no need to fear.

In Psalm 62:6–7 David wrote, "He only is my rock and my salvation: he is my defence; I shall not be moved. In God is my salvation and my glory: the rock of my strength, and my refuge, is in God." Also, in Psalm 40:1–2 David wrote, "I waited patiently for the Lord; and he inclined unto me, and heard my cry. He brought me up also out of an horrible pit, out of the mercy clay, and set my feet upon a rock, and established my goings."

The secret of a secure life is faith in the Lord Jesus Christ who becomes our rock. Even though there are troubling events taking place all around us, the person who can walk with certainty is the person who is standing on Jesus Christ the Rock.

THE ROAD TO THE WATERFALL

On the way to the church there is a road sign that says "Sugao Waterfall." Although I have lived in this area for over thirty years, I had never been to see the waterfall. However, our son-in-law had seen a picture of the waterfall on the Internet, so he wanted to go to see it.

One morning we headed off in search of the waterfall. We got lost along the way, so I stopped and asked a hiker for directions. After giving us directions, he warned me, "It's a very narrow road." His warning was correct. The road to the waterfall was quite narrow, and the closer we got to the waterfall, the more narrow the road became. Finally, it became a road just barely wide enough for one car.

My family became quite nervous, but I kept repeating, "It's okay. It's okay." The truth is no one in the car was more nervous than I was. After all, you could put your hand out the window and touch large boulders on the left side of the car and tree limbs on the right side of the car.

Finally, we came to a spot too narrow for the car, so we got out and walked the rest of the way to the falls. In about four or five minutes the falls came into sight. There were actually three waterfalls, and the instant we saw them, we forgot all about our tension of a few minutes earlier. It was a majestic sight.

As Christians walk the road of life, from time to time the road becomes extremely narrow. There are troubles on the left side of the road and trials on the right side. However, if we will trust the Lord and continue walking, we shall discover that there is great value in walking the path of faith. There may be times when we think, "I want to quit this walk. I don't want to go any further," but if we rely on the help of the Lord, eventually we shall be able to see a spectacle many times more majestic than a waterfall. It is the spectacle of the country of God Himself, and when we stand before Him and hear Him say, "Well done, thou good and faithful servant" (Matthew 25:23), we'll forget all of the troubles and trials along the way.

Ken Board

OUR DAUGHTER AND
THE SUPERHERO

In the morning our daughter would usually watch children's programs, but in the afternoon she liked to watch the Japanese superhero programs like *Shaida* and *Jasupion*. I don't know why, but she especially like *Shaida*. I bought her a book about *Shaida* and a cassette tape with the *Shaida* theme song on it. Later I wished I hadn't bought it because she listened to that tape over and over again while looking at the book and nearly drove me crazy.

One day there was a *Shaida* show at the shopping center, so we took our daughter to see it. First, several bad guys came out and frightened the children, but Shaida appeared and chased them away. After the show there was a time for autographs and photographs. When we took our daughter's picture with Shaida, he gave her a hug. I'll never forget the look on our daughter's face when she met Shaida face to face.

Although I've never met my "superhero," the Lord Jesus Christ, face-to-face, I believe in Him and love Him. "Whom having not see, ye love; in whom, though now ye see him not, yet believing, ye rejoice with joy unspeakable and full of glory" (1 Peter 1:8). Not only that, according to 1 John 3:2, "we shall see him as he is." In fact, Revelation 22:4 clearly states, "And they shall see his face."

Wow! Can you imagine the joy of our hearts when we look into the face of the Savior who died on the cross for our sins! I can imagine it, for I saw that joy on the face of my daughter when she was hugged by Shaida.

THE BLIND LADY AND THE CAVE

The afternoon of the second day of summer camp was set aside for recreation. The pastor took the young people to an obstacle course while I took the older folks to explore a large cave. One of the ladies that went with us was a blind lady. There are several narrow, slippery places in the cave and the ceiling is very low in spots, so I was concerned that she might be injured. However, she grasped the arm of one of the ladies, and, doing exactly as the lady told her to do, she walked carefully over the slippery places and bowed her head at the low places, so she came out of the cave unharmed.

I was the one who ended up getting hurt. Because I was able to make it all the way to the end of the cave safely, I became overconfident on my way back. I became engrossed in a discussion with another missionary and cracked my head on one of the low ceilings. The blind lady was fine, but I walked out of the cave with blood flowing from the wound in my head.

The Christian who is able to walk the path of faith safely is the Christian who, because he is aware of his own weakness, clings to the Lord and follows His guidance. There is a wonderful promise of the Lord written in Isaiah 42:16: "And I will bring the blind by a way that they knew not; I will lead them in paths that they have not known: I will make darkness light before them, and crooked things straight. These things will I do unto them, and not forsake them."

When we are walking blindly, let's watch out for those low ceilings and hang onto the Lord, who will always bring us out safely.

Ken Board

POOR BROTHER DAVE

All of us were blessed by the ministry of Brother Dave at our Music Camp. Brother Dave and his wife were also greatly blessed through their fellowship with the Christians of the churches in Kyushu.

However, Brother Dave had to put up with two big problems while he was in Japan. The first problem was the low ceilings in many buildings in Japan. Brother Dave is over six feet tall, so wherever we went—church, restaurants, rest rooms, trains—he was constantly bumping his head.

The other problem was the custom in Japan to drive on the left side of the road. When I pulled out of the airport parking lot onto the left side of the road, Brother Dave actually stood up in the seat and began to motion frantically for me to get over to the right. He must have thought he was about to die in an automobile accident.

Every time we went somewhere in the car, he would try to enter on the driver's side. I kept asking him, "Are you driving?" Finally, he became accustomed to driving on the left side of the road during his last couple of days in Japan. However, this presented him with another problem. When he returned to America, he would immediately have to get used to driving on the right side of the road again.

Just as Brother Dave had a hard time conforming to life in Japan because of his height and the customs, Christians have become people who no longer conform to this world because of their faith in Christ. In the gospel of John, Christ explained the relationship of believers and this world: "I have given them thy word; and the world hath hated them, because they are not of the world, even as I am not of the world" (17:14).

If we who are not of this world are able to live in this world without trouble, perhaps it is because we are trying too hard to conform to the customs of this world.

THE HALF-WASHED CAR

It was Wednesday afternoon and there were two things I wanted to accomplish. I wanted to wash my car, and I wanted to finish preparing my Wednesday evening message, so even though there actually wasn't enough time to do both things, I hurriedly washed my car and then hurriedly finished my message.

Later when I went to get into the car to go to church, I noticed that because I had washed the car so hurriedly, I had really washed only about half of it. Furthermore, when I preached my message, because I had prepared it so hurriedly, it wasn't nearly as effective as usual.

The half-washed car and the half-prepared message symbolize the mistake of some Christians who are tempted to do so many things that everything they do ends up half done. Whether it is a job or housework, anything that is only half-done will sooner or later become an embarrassment, just as I was embarrassed to drive to church in a half-washed car and preach a half-prepared message; however, if the work that we are trying to accomplish is work for the Lord, a half-done job is more than just mere embarrassment. It is a serious mistake.

When the Lord leads us to do a certain task, we ought to put our full effort into completing that task. Paul's words in Philippians 3:13, "This one thing I do," manifest one of the secrets of the success of his ministry. According to verse 14 of the same chapter, Paul "pressed toward the mark."

Let's ask the Lord, "What is the one thing you want me to do right now? What is the mark toward which you want me to press?" When the Lord reveals that "one thing" to us, let's be careful of becoming so busy with various other activities that we end up doing only half of the work that the Lord entrusted to us.

Ken Board

THE BAG ON MY HEAD

A missionary friend and his son went with me to see a baseball game. Two days before, our local team had lost 11-4 and then the next day they lost again, this time by a 10-3 score. We didn't think they would lose that badly three days in a row, but just in case, we each took a certain item with us.

When the opponents jumped out to a 9-2 lead and it became obvious that our team was about to suffer another embarrassing defeat, the three of us took out some brown bags with two holes cut out for our eyes and put them over our heads. When the fans sitting around us saw the bags on our heads, they began laughing loudly. Several people took out their cell phones and took photos of us.

Of course, everyone knew the meaning of the bags. We were saying, "We are getting sick of watching this team play this kind of baseball. We are ashamed to be fans of this team."

The image of us with the bags on our heads is the image of some Christians. They believe in Christ but are ashamed to confess their faith publicly. Just as the three of us hid our faces, these Christians are hiding their faith in Christ. However, according to the Bible, those who believe in Christ are going to gain the victory, so there is no need at all to be ashamed. Let's boldly confess the fact that we are Christians to our family and friends.

Paul declared, "For I am not ashamed of the gospel of Christ" (Romans 1:16). Let us too declare to everyone, "I am not ashamed of being a Christian."

Let us proclaim with Paul, "According to my earnest expectation, and my hope, that in nothing I shall be ashamed, but that with all boldness, as always, so now also Christ shall be magnified in my body, whether it be by life, or by death" (Philippians 1:20).

THREE PIECES OF CANDY

During the ladies' meeting at summer camp, some of the children who came into the class with their mothers became restless, so my wife gave each one some candy.

When she placed three pieces of candy on the table in front of one little boy, he grabbed one with his right hand and one with his left hand. He wanted the remaining piece too, so he put the one in his right hand into his mouth and picked up the third piece of candy; however, the piece he put into his mouth was too big, so he laid the piece in his right hand on the table and used that hand to take the piece out of his mouth. He had a piece of candy in each hand, but his eyes were fixed on the piece of candy on the table. Once more he put the one in his right hand into his mouth and picked up the third piece of candy. He repeated this action several times. It was quite amusing to watch.

Sitting there with one piece of candy in his right hand and one piece of candy in his left hand and a third piece of candy in his mouth, that little boy was the perfect image of the life of a Christian. Although there are times of trial and adversity, the life of a Christian is a life overflowing with peace and joy. Some people have the idea that the Christian life is boring. They couldn't be any more mistaken. The Christian life resembles a little boy with a piece of candy in each hand and one more in his mouth. The words of David in Psalm 23 show us the true picture of the Christian life, especially the words in verse 5: "My cup runneth over."

The Christian has peace in his right hand, joy in his left hand, and praise in his mouth. How could a life like this ever be boring?

Ken Board

"SHE" AND "HE"

We were talking in the car on our way home from the shopping center when my wife asked me, "Did she say when he was coming?" It was a question that had nothing to do with the subject about which we had just been talking, so I was totally confused. I asked her, "Who is 'she' and who is 'he'?"

She explained, "You remember. Yesterday when we went to the Christian bookstore to buy the plaque with a Bible passage engraved on it. They didn't have the one we wanted, so the girl at the store told us that she would have the store deliveryman bring it to us as soon as it arrived."

In her mind my wife had been thinking about that conversation, but because I could not read her mind, I had no idea what in the world she was talking about when she suddenly asked me, "Did she say when he was coming?" When we suddenly blurt out a question about something we have been pondering in our mind, it would be helpful to the other person to explain the context of our words.

This principle also holds true in regard to the Bible. When we want to understand the meaning of a passage, it is a mistake to ignore the relationship of that passage with the words that precede it and follow it. In fact, ignoring the context of a passage is a mistake that leads to many heresies. I suppose the most well-known example is the humorous tale of the man who opened his Bible and read, "Judas went and hanged himself."

He closed his Bible and opened it to another passage, which read, "Go, and do thou likewise."

He closed his Bible, then opened it to another passage which read, "What thou doest, do quickly."

Christians, let's be careful. Even the Devil can quote the Bible (Matthew 4). When someone from a cult starts quoting Scripture to us, let's open our Bible and study the entire context and find out who "he" and "she" and "I" and "they" really are.

"Study to shew thyself approved unto God, a workman that needeth not to be ashamed, rightly dividing the word of truth" (2 Timothy 2:15).

THE SUMO WRESTLER'S MISSTEP

There a game that I like to play on the Internet. It's a sumo game. It's quite simple. Every other month there is a fifteen-day sumo tournament. Each day during the tournament I choose ten wrestlers that I think will win that day and I have an opponent who does the same. Whoever chooses the most winners is declared the victor for that day. (There is no cash or prizes involved.)

Through the first twelve days of this month's tournament, my record was seven wins and five losses. However, it should have been eight wins and four losses. The other day one of the wrestlers that I had chosen quickly grabbed his opponent's belt and marched him out of the ring. However, the referee raised the hand of the other wrestler.

I jumped from my chair and yelled, "You're wrong! You're wrong! My guy won!" My windows were open, so I'm certain the neighbors all wondered what in the world was going on at my house.

There are five judges who sit around the ring and make certain the referee's decision is correct. When they announced that these judges would review the match, I sat down in my chair and relaxed, for I was certain that these judges would overturn the decision of the referee. When they announced that the wrestler that I had chosen had inadvertently stepped out of the ring before he shoved his opponent out and therefore the decision of the referee was correct, I jumped out of my chair again. "Stepped out of the ring? What are you talking about? He didn't step out of the ring!" Later they showed a replay of the match, and sure enough, my guy had stepped out of the ring a second before he shoved his opponent out.

In life, too, sometimes victory or defeat may depend on one small misstep. Just when we think we've won, we get careless, and our enemy gains the victory. The night the Lord Jesus was arrested, Peter boldly bragged, "Though all men shall be offended because of thee, yet will I never be offended" (Matthew 26:33). But later there was a misstep in the actions of Peter. He sat with the enemies of Christ and put himself in a situation where he had to deny the Lord in order to save his own life.

In 1 Corinthians 10:12 the Bible says, "Wherefore let him that thinketh he standeth take heed lest he fall." To put it in the words of the world of sumo, "Let him who thinks he is winning be careful of a misstep."

Ken Board

TEETH? NERVES? EARS? SHOULDER? NECK?

One afternoon the right side of my face began to hurt. That night the pain was so bad that I could hardly sleep. When I awoke, it hurt even more, so I concluded that it was a toothache and went to the dentist. The dentist examined my teeth, took some X-rays, and told me, "Your teeth are fine. Maybe it is a nerve problem. I am going to send you to a nerve specialist."

The nerve specialist at the huge hospital ran several tests and announced, "It's not your nerves. Maybe it's your ears. Go see an ear specialist."

The ear specialist examined my ears and took some X-rays and said, "Your ears are fine. Maybe it's your neck or shoulder. I am going to send you to an orthopedist."

By now I had heard enough, so I went home without going to the orthopedist. I felt like the woman in the eighth chapter of Luke who "had spent all her living upon physicians, neither could be healed of any" (verse 43).

Just as I was desperately seeking a doctor who could ease my pain, there are many people in the world who run to and fro desperately seeking someone or something that can heal the pain of their hearts. They run to sports, pleasure, fortune-tellers, religion, money, education, work, psychiatrists, and friends. They plead, "Please heal my heart," but they are unable to find anyone or anything that can ease the pain of their heart.

There is only one person who can heal the heart of man. That one person is the "Great Physician," the Lord Jesus Christ. In Luke 4:18 Jesus said, "The Spirit of the Lord is upon me; He hath sent me to heal the broken-hearted." Christ alone has the power to heal the wounds of the heart. The broken-hearted person who will trust in the healing power of the Lord Jesus will be given a clean, new heart.

"Therefore if any man be in Christ, he is a new creature: old things are passed away; behold, all things are become new" (2 Corinthians 5:17).

UH-OH

When I visited our missionary to Taiwan, I was amused by a radar sensor in his car. (This is allowed in Taiwan.) On many of the main roads there are cameras that take pictures of cars driving faster than the speed limit. Because the missionary has a radar sensor in his car, if he is going over the speed limit when he approaches one of those cameras, the device will warn him.

Of course, the warning is in Chinese, so I couldn't understand what the device was saying. However, I did recognize one word. In a girl's cute voice, the device would say, "Uh-oh." I don't know why, but I really took a liking to that voice. Every now and then I would deliberately have the missionary drive over the speed limit so I could hear, "Uh-oh." It became a joke between him and me. Even now when I call him and he answers the phone, I don't say, "Hello." I say, "Uh-oh," and he replies with laughter, "Uh-oh."

Did you know that there is a warning device like that in every church? It's called "the pastor." When the spiritual condition of a church has gone down, it is the job of the pastor to warn the church: "Uh-oh." In 1 Thessalonians 5:14 Paul wrote, "Now we exhort you, brethren, warn them that are unruly."

Of course, the pastor's voice will not be a cute voice like the voice in the device in the missionary's car. In fact, it may be a loud voice that rebukes us or a soft, tear-filled appeal. For three years Paul warned the elders of Ephesus day and night with tears (Acts 20:31).

Whether it is a voice that rebukes the entire church or a voice that warns just one member, when we hear the pastor saying "Uh-oh," let's listen carefully to his voice.

Ken Board

THE WEIRD-LOOKING GUY

On Saturday one of the church members headed for the church. As she neared the church, she spotted a weird-looking man in front of the church. He was wearing a Los Angeles Dodgers baseball cap, he needed a shave, his shirt was hanging out of his trousers, and he had on old, worn-out shoes. She didn't realize it at first, but I was that weird-looking guy.

That lady saw what I normally look like on Saturdays. There are two reasons why I dress like that on Saturday. First, I usually do yard work on Saturday. Second, I want to relax and be comfortable on Saturday. Because I am in the ministry, every day except Saturday I shave, comb my hair, and wear nice clothing in case I meet someone I know. However, at least one day during the week I want to be able to forget about shaving, put on my Dodger hat, put on some comfortable clothes and shoes, and feel relaxed.

Of course, I never dress that way when I go to church on Sunday. On Sunday without fail I shave, comb my hair, brush my teeth, and put on a white shirt and tie. The only image of me that most of the church members have seen is my Sunday image. That's why the church member didn't recognize me when she saw my Saturday image.

Just as I have a both a Sunday image and a Saturday image, all people have an outward appearance and an inward appearance. Even though their outward appearance may be splendid, their inward appearance before God may be similar to my Saturday image. The Lord Jesus said to the scribes and Pharisees, "Even so ye also outwardly appear righteous unto men, but within ye are full of hypocrisy and iniquity" (Matthew 23:28).

When we go to church on Sunday, our outward appearance may be impressive, but what about the appearance of our heart? Is it similar to the weird-looking guy that the church member saw in front of the church? If we are outwardly righteous but inwardly unrighteous, let's remember the solemn words of Christ written in Luke 16:15: "Ye are they which justify yourselves before men; but God knoweth your hearts."

VINEGAR! VIN-E-GAR!

He pulled up in front of our house in a small truck. The veteran missionary had told us that he would come by selling mayonnaise, ketchup, vinegar, and other such items. We had just arrived in Japan and spoke no Japanese, and he spoke almost no English. My wife said to him, "I want some vinegar."

He didn't understand. She said it again, slowly, "I want some vinegar." He didn't understand.

She thought, "Maybe if I say the word more slowly, he will understand," so she said, "Vinegar! Vin-e-gar!"

It was obvious that they weren't communicating, so my wife thought, "I will go out to the truck with him and show him."

When she said, "I'll show you," his eyes lit up and he exclaimed, "Oh, you want some *shooyu*!" At the time, we didn't know it, but the Japanese word for soy sauce is *shooyu*, which is pronounced just like the English words *show you*, so when my wife said, "I'll show you," he quickly ran to his truck and brought back a large bottle of soy sauce. My wife just gave up and bought the soy sauce.

There were a lot of misunderstandings like this our first couple of years in Japan, but no one should ever misunderstand the meaning of the words of the Lord Jesus written in the Bible, for He introduced Himself to us with simple words that even a child can understand.

"I am the bread of life" (John 6:35).

"I am the light of the world" (John 8:12).

"I am the door" (John 10:9).

"I am the way" (John 14:6).

"Bread, light, door, way"—all four of these words are one-syllable words. While a person in Japan might not understand if you are talking about vinegar or soy sauce, no one would misunderstand the words that Christ used to explain the salvation that he gives, so it is not understanding that is needed for salvation. It is simple faith in Christ. "Believe on the Lord Jesus Christ, and thou shalt be saved" (Acts 16:31).

Ken Board

THE TARTAR SAUCE
IN MY POCKET

About once a month I enjoy having lunch at a local Chinese restaurant. I can choose two out of five dishes, and soup, rice, and Japanese pickles come with the meal. I always order the same thing: shrimp and sweet-and-sour pork. The sweet-and-sour pork is very delicious.

The shrimp is delicious too, but the restaurant doesn't have any tartar sauce or ketchup. I like lots of tartar sauce on my shrimp, so whenever I go to eat at that restaurant, I put a small container of tartar sauce in my pocket. When my meal comes, I wait until no one is looking and take the tartar sauce out of my pocket and pour it all over the shrimp. When I do so, the flavor of the shrimp is so much better. Because of the tartar sauce in my pocket, I look forward to eating at that restaurant.

Just as the tartar sauce in my pocket makes my meal more enjoyable, the Word of God stored in the heart of a Christian makes his Christian life more enjoyable. There are times when adversities and trials weaken the flavor of our faith, but when we remember the Word of God that we have stored in our hearts, those words once again bring a savory flavor to our Christian life.

In Psalm 119:11 it is written, "Thy word have I hid in mine heart, that I might not sin against thee." Being able to avoid sins against the Lord is a good result of storing the Word of God in our hearts, but it is not the only reward. There is also the reward of our daily Christian life becoming a savory life to which we can look forward with delight. "How sweet are thy words unto my taste! Yea, sweeter than honey to my mouth!" (Psalm 119:103).

THE TEAKETTLE THAT LOST ITS WHISTLE

I love to start off the day with the morning newspaper and a cup of hot coffee. As soon as I arise, I put water into the teakettle and turn on the stove. Then I go get the newspaper out of the mailbox and sit down to read it while I'm waiting for the water to boil.

When I read the newspaper, I read every headline on every page, and if I see a headline that arouses my interest, I read the entire article. Just about the time that I reach my favorite section of the newspaper—the sports section—I will hear the whistle of the teakettle and get up and go into the kitchen and fix my coffee.

One morning I was already finished reading the sports section when I realized that I hadn't heard the teakettle whistle yet, so I went to the kitchen to check on it. The water was already boiling, but the whistle was silent. I examined the teakettle closely and discovered that the rubber top of the whistle had melted, and as a result, the teakettle could no longer whistle.

If Christians are not careful, the fire of adversity may cause us to lose our voice of praise to the Lord. That's what happened to the people of Israel when they were taken into captivity. "For there they that carried us away captive required of us a song; and they that wasted us required of us mirth, saying, Sing us one of the songs of Zion" (Psalm 137:3). The sorrowful reply of the people of Israel is recorded in verse 4: "How shall we sing the Lord's song in a strange land?"

Of course there will be times when we will have to walk through the valley of the fiery trial, but instead of ending up like my teakettle that lost its whistle, let's continue to rejoice in the Lord and praise His name. "Beloved, think it not strange concerning the fiery trial which is to try you, as though some strange thing happened unto you. But rejoice, inasmuch as ye are partakers of Christ's suffering; that, when his glory shall be revealed, ye may be glad also with exceeding joy" (1 Peter 4:12–13).

Even in the time of trial, let's lift up our hearts and sing the Lord's song in a voice that can be heard by everyone around us.

Ken Board

A4 AND B5

Last week's sermon turned out to be much longer than usual. Let me tell you why.

When I prepare a sermon in Japanese, I don't prepare just an outline. I write out the entire message. Then I print it on B5 paper and cut it to the same size as my Bible. For a while I had been preparing ten pages of notes, but the sermons were rather long, so recently I had reduced the message to seven pages.

When I prepared last week's message, I prepared seven pages of notes, just as I always do. However, when I put the B5 paper in my printer and clicked on "print," I was surprised to see that the paper was too small. Only about half of the content of each page would fit on the paper. I wondered what was going on, but then I thought, "Maybe . . ." I checked the settings on my computer, and just as I had suspected, I had forgotten to change the paper size from A4 to B5. When I reset the computer to B5 and printed my message, my seven-page message turned into a long eleven-page message.

Many of the plans of man unexpectedly end up in failure. We decide on a goal, and make specific plans in order to reach that goal. We work hard to achieve the goal. However, if there is illness or loss of employment or an accident, we see our plans crumble before our eyes. It is only when our plans are in unity with God's plan that we can be assured of accomplishing our goals.

In Proverbs 3:5–6 the Bible says, "Trust in the Lord with all thine heart; and lean not unto thine own understanding. In all thy ways acknowledge him, and he shall direct thy paths." Or, we could say, "In all thy ways acknowledge him, and you won't have to worry that B5 turns out to be A4."

THE STRANGE EAR DOCTOR

Lately I have been troubled by a ringing in my ears, so I went to an ear doctor. Of course, I assumed that the first thing he would do would be to examine my ears. However, without even glancing at my ears, first of all he tested my hearing in a soundproof room. Next, he asked me several questions. After hearing my answers, he wrote a prescription and sent me home.

It was the same the second time I went and also the third time. He has been treating my ears for about a month now, but he has yet to look at my ears even one time. In the past when I went to an ear doctor, the first thing he did was look at my ears. It's different now. Ear doctors seem to rely entirely on machines and the words of the patient to make a diagnosis. I am not used to this method, so this ear doctor seems quite strange to me.

The ear doctor may listen to the words of the patient and diagnose the problem, but God's method of diagnosis is different. When God diagnoses our spiritual condition, He always looks at our heart first. According to 1 Samuel 16:7, "Man looketh on the outward appearance, but the Lord looketh on the heart."

We may try to deceive the Lord with our eloquent words, but the Lord ignores those words and immediately checks our heart. Every time we pray, we ought to remember, "The Lord is looking at my heart." The words of David in Psalm 26:2 show us the proper attitude of prayer: "Examine me, O Lord, and prove me; try my reins and my heart."

Ken Board

THE TRIP I DIDN'T WANT TO MAKE

I had made up my mind to attend my friend's wedding, but when I thought about the pain in my feet (I have neuropathy), I really didn't want to make the trip all the way to Toyama Prefecture from Kyushu. I would go by plane from Fukuoka to Komatsu, so that wasn't a problem, but from Komatsu to Kosugi I would have to go by train, and I knew that would involve a lot of walking at the train station.

After I boarded the plane, I was reading a newspaper as I waited for the plane to depart. Suddenly, someone touched my shoulder and said, "Pastor Board." When I looked up, I saw a young lady who used to attend one of the churches I had started. After we landed at Komatsu, she asked me, "How are you going to get to Kosugi? A friend of mine who lives in Kosugi is coming to meet me. Would you like to ride with us?" Her friend drove me all the way to the front door of my friend's home, so I even had time that evening to have supper with him.

After the wedding the next day I would have to take the train from Kosugi to Komatsu, so again I was dreading the trip. However, a missionary friend who planned to go right by the Komatsu airport on his way home offered to give me a ride, so not only was I able to avoid the painful walking, I also had the opportunity to enjoy good fellowship with the missionary and his family for over an hour.

When I arrived home, I thanked the Lord. "Lord, not only did you protect my way, you also made it possible for me to have fellowship with my friends!"

In our Christian journey there are times when we have to take a path that we don't want to walk. As we imagine the suffering of that path, we sense unpleasant feelings. At those times let's remember the promise of the Lord, who has already provided blessings along the way. "Have not I commanded thee? Be strong and of a good courage; be not afraid, neither be thou dismayed: for the Lord thy God is with thee whithersoever thou goest" (Joshua 1:9).

THE WHITE MOUSE

Our daughter's cry, "Daddy! Daddy!" woke me up. I looked at the clock and saw that it was 3:50. Groaning, I got out of bed, walked to her room, turned on the light, and asked, "What's wrong?"

She replied, "There's a white mouse in my room."

I knew it was not likely that a white mouse was in her room, but then I thought, "Maybe her hamster escaped from its cage." Nope, the hamster was sleeping soundly in its cage. I searched all over our daughter's room and the next room, but there was no white mouse. When I told her that there was no white mouse, she relaxed and was asleep again in just a few minutes. I wish I could have gone back to sleep right away, but I was awake for quite a while.

Our daughter was afraid of a white mouse that wasn't there. Likewise, many people are fearing some sort of "white mouse." They are similar to the people described in Proverbs: "The wicked flee when no man pursueth" (28:1).

According to Luke 21:26, the time will come when the hearts of men shall fail them for fear. Even now, the hearts of many people are controlled by the fear of events that may or may not take place. Of course, the "white mouse" that is the cause of that fear will differ from person to person, but their fear is an unnecessary fear.

When we trust in the Lord, He protects us from needless fear. In 2 Timothy 1:7 Paul wrote, "For God hath not given us the spirit of fear; but of power, and of love, and of a sound mind."

My daughter relaxed when she heard me say, "There's no white mouse in your room." Christians too should be at ease when we hear the words of the Lord: "Fear thou not; for I am with thee: be not dismayed; for I am thy God: I will strengthen thee; yea, I will help thee; yea, I will uphold thee with the right hand of my righteousness" (Isaiah 41:10).

And even if there is a "white mouse" in our room, because we know that the Lord is with us, there is no need to fear.

Ken Board

THE LOOK ON THE LITTLE BOY'S FACE

I was on my way home and ended up in a long line of traffic waiting at a red light. I looked around and saw a small boy standing at the entrance to a supermarket. As people neared the entrance of the store, they would step on the mat and the door would open automatically. Finally, the boy decided to give it a try himself. He stepped on the mat and the door opened. His eyes grew large and his face was filled with wonder and amazement.

He stepped off the mat and the door closed. For a couple of minutes he just stood there staring at the door, and then he stepped on the mat again, and the door opened. He stepped off and the door closed. He then proceeded to step on and off the mat several times, each time reacting with amazement at his power to open and close the door. I sat there watching his face until finally the traffic moved and I had to go. The last time I saw him, he was still standing there staring at the door with a look of wonder on his face.

The actions and reactions of that small boy picture the life of a Christian. According to 2 Peter 1:4: "whereby are given unto us exceeding great and precious promises." When we believe those promises and test their reality, our heart is filled with wonder and amazement like the face of that little boy. Over and over again we marvel at the power of God to open doors for us. When we need the help of the Lord, let's step by faith on His promises, and experience a Christian life filled with wonder and amazement.

The Amusings of a Missionary

"BROTHER SAKAI!"

I noticed that the light in one of the rooms at church was flickering on and off, so I unscrewed it and took a look at it. I could tell it was rather old, so I walked to the store just down the street, bought a new light, walked back to church, and screwed the new light into place. The light didn't come on. I worked with the light a while trying to get it to come on, and then my wife and two other ladies each took turns trying to get the light to work without any success, so the four of us just stood there wondering what to do.

I thought, "I wish Brother Sakai were here right now. He can repair anything electrical." Suddenly, just as if Brother Sakai were in the next room and could hear my voice, I shouted, "Brother Sakai!"

You may find this hard to believe, but in that instant the light came on. It was almost as if Brother Sakai had come racing into the room and repaired the light, but he wasn't even in Kyushu at the time. The four of us laughed in amazement.

The Bible teaches in Romans 10:13 that the instant a person who is seeking salvation calls upon the name of the Lord, that person is saved. "For whosoever shall call upon the name of the Lord shall be saved." Psalm 86:5 says this about the Lord: "For thou, Lord, art good, and ready to forgive: and plenteous in mercy unto all them that call upon thee." Furthermore, in Jeremiah 33:3 the Lord says, "Call unto me, and I will answer thee."

If you are not a Christian yet, give it a try. Just call upon the name of the Lord with words something like this: "Lord, I am a sinner. I believe that Jesus Christ died on the cross for my sins. I now repent of my sins and receive the Lord Jesus as my personal Savior. Please forgive my sins and save my soul." If you will pray this prayer from your heart, just as quickly as the light came on when I shouted Brother Sakai's name, you will become a child of God who can go to heaven.

Ken Board

THE CAR IN THE MIRROR

I was tired. I had driven home from Oita (three–four hours) earlier in the day, preached in the Wednesday evening service, taken several people home, and now was on my way home with my family. I came to an intersection where there was no signal. There was a mirror, however, and I saw the headlights of an oncoming car in the mirror, so I stopped and waited.

Several seconds passed and the car didn't come, so I moved forward a little, and when I did, the other car moved forward a little. I stopped my car and waited several seconds, but the other car didn't come. I became quite annoyed and shouted, "Where is he? Why doesn't he come on? What in the world is he waiting for?"

I moved forward again and so did the other car. I was becoming more and more irritated by the second. Just then I realized that the car in the mirror was my own car! I was waiting on myself. I was irritated at myself.

My behavior that night mirrors the behavior of many people. Like Adam and Eve in the garden of Eden, they have a tendency to blame other people for all of their problems. When God asked Adam, "Hast thou eaten of the tree, whereof I commanded thee that thou shouldest not eat?" Adam blamed it on Eve. "The woman whom thou gavest to be with me, she gave me of the tree, and I did eat." When God asked the woman, "What is this that thou hast done?" the woman blamed it on the serpent. "The serpent beguiled me, and I did eat" (Genesis 3:11–13).

When we are angry with other people and blame them for all of our problems, it could be that the real problem lies in the person that we see in the mirror.

CHOSEN OUT OF 28,827

"I am Mr. Katoh from RKB," he said as he sat down beside me. (RKB is one of the local radio stations.) I had promised a missionary's son that I would take him to a baseball game at Yahoo Dome if he passed his high school entrance exam, so that's where I was when Mr. Katoh suddenly appeared. We began a conversation that consisted mainly of his questions and my answers. He wanted to know information such as how long I had been in Japan and which Hawks' player was my favorite.

He then startled me by saying, "I'd like you to say a few words on the radio." I was quite nervous, but I went on the live broadcast and talked about baseball for twenty to thirty seconds.

There were 28,827 fans at Yahoo Dome that night. I wonder why Mr. Katoh chose me. Maybe it was because I was a foreigner speaking Japanese. Maybe it was because I was cheering fanatically for the Hawks. Maybe it was because almost everyone sitting around me was watching the game quietly, so I stood out. I didn't bother to ask him, but for some reason I was chosen out of 28,827 people.

According to the Bible, all people who believe in Christ are "chosen." In Ephesians 1:4 it is written, "According as he hath chosen us in him before the foundation of the world." The word *chosen* does not refer to an arbitrary decision of God to save some people and consign other people to hell. A God who would make that sort of arbitrary decision would be a cruel God, not a God of love.

The passage that explains the meaning of the word *chosen* is 1 Peter 1:2: "elect according to the foreknowledge of God the Father." This passage teaches us that God chose us according to His foreknowledge. In other words, knowing before the foundation of the world that we would believe in the Lord Jesus Christ, God chose us on the basis of His omniscience.

Every person has the freedom to choose to receive Christ or to choose to reject Christ. However, the person who makes the decision to receive Christ as personal Savior discovers the wonderful truth that he is one of God's chosen people. "Ye have not chosen me, but I have chosen you" (John 15:16).

Ken Board

DIY AND FIY

Here and there are stores that have the letters DIY written on their signs. Of course, DIY stands for "Do It Yourself." DIY stores are for people who like to take care of matters regarding their homes and cars by themselves because it's much cheaper than hiring a professional.

When we took our daughter and her husband to our son's home in Kagoshima, they really liked the musical clock in his home, so they asked, "Where did you buy that?"

He meant to reply, "At a nearby DIY store," but he made a mistake and said, "At a nearby FIY store."

After laughing for a while I asked him, "I know about DIY stores, but what is an FIY store?"

Our sharp-witted son replied, "It's a Fix It Yourself store."

I suppose that if you have the ability to remodel your house or repair your car, a DIY store would be of help, but when it comes to the salvation of a person's soul, DIY will not get the job done. According to the Bible, there is not one thing a person can do to save himself. In Titus 3:5 the Bible says, "Not by works of righteousness which we have done, but according to his mercy he saved us, by the washing of regeneration, and renewing of the Holy Ghost."

On the other hand, after a person becomes a Christian, FIY is not only helpful but also necessary. When a Christian realizes that he has sinned and gone away from the Lord, if he will pray to the Lord and confess his sins, he can repair the broken fellowship between himself and the Lord. "If we confess our sins, he is faithful and just to forgive us our sins, and to cleanse us from all unrighteousness" (1 John 1:9).

THE PASTOR DISAPPEARED

When we moved my son's belongings to Kokubu, we went in three vehicles. My wife rode with my son in the lead car. My daughter and a pastor friend's daughter rode with me in the truck. The pastor and his wife followed in my van. When we exited the expressway near Kokubu, I checked to make certain that the pastor had followed me. My son paid his toll, pulled over to the right, and waited. I paid my toll, pulled behind my son's car, and waited. There was no rearview mirror in the truck, so I checked both side mirrors and couldn't see the pastor anywhere.

The longer I waited, the more impatient I became. I said to my daughter, "He was right behind me when we left the expressway. Where in the world did he go?" After a while I asked my daughter to get out and see if she could spot the pastor anywhere. She was back in just a couple of seconds. "He's right behind you," she said. All that time we had been waiting for the pastor, he was sitting behind us, but he had stopped the van in a spot where he was right behind me, so I couldn't see him in either of the side mirrors.

There are times in the Christian life when we feel like getting off the expressway of life and checking to see if the Lord is still with us. We become anxious and exclaim, "Where did the Lord go? Has He forsaken me?" No, He has not left us. In Matthew 28:20 He promised, "I am with you always." In John 6:37 there is another wonderful promise: "Him that cometh to me I will in no wise cast out." As if these two promises were not enough, Hebrews 13:5 quotes these words of God: "I will never leave thee, nor forsake thee."

On the way home from Kokubu I had the pastor drive in front of my van so there would be no repetition of the incident. Let's do the same in our Christian lives. If we let the Lord go in front and follow Him, there will no longer be any need to fret and worry.

Ken Board

THE BUS IN THE RIVER

When I saw the picture in the newspaper, I laughed for several minutes. It was so funny. The picture was a picture of a bus that had fallen into a river. The bus driver and nine passengers were on the bus when it fell into the river, but no one was hurt. Of course, a bus that has fallen into a river would not normally be something about which we would laugh. However, the bus that had fallen into the river was a driving-school bus! The nine passengers were all students of the driving school.

I imagine that the driving school was quite embarrassed over this incident. How about it? If you wanted to send your son or daughter to driving school, would you send them to that school? I think I would look for another school.

When this sort of incident takes place at church, it is no laughing matter. In fact, it is a sad occasion. When a Christian falls into sin, often it becomes an incident that brings shame to his church. The fallen Christian and his church become objects of scorn and laughter.

Of course, each Christian should testify of his faith to his family and friends, but there is a great responsibility that accompanies that testimony. It is his responsibility to live a life that is worthy of his testimony, for when the people around him see the sin in his life, they will not think well of him or his church.

In Ephesians 4:1 the apostle Paul wrote, "Walk worthy of the vocation wherewith ye are called." Therefore, let's follow the admonition in 2 Timothy 2:19: "Let every one that nameth the name of Christ depart from iniquity."

FIRST GEAR WAS REVERSE AND SECOND GEAR WAS FIRST GEAR!

I rented a truck to help my son move to Kokubu. When I got into the truck, I put it into First Gear and stepped on the gas. To my amazement the truck went backward. I looked at the gear markings carefully and I knew I was in trouble. The first gear on the left in my car is First and the second gear on the left is Second, but on the truck the first gear on the left was Reverse and the second gear on the left was First Gear. If this sounds confusing to you, imagine how confusing it was to me.

I was able to drive the truck safely from the rental truck parking lot to my son's apartment in Kokubu, but it was a very dangerous trip. Every time I stopped at a red light, I would put the truck into first gear, and when the light turned green, the truck would go backward. A pastor friend was following me in his car, and several times he had to blow his horn at me to stop me from colliding with his car. I drove the truck to Kokubu and back (about 350 miles), but I never did get used to the gears. Just before I returned the truck, I stopped at a gas station, and when I started to pull away from the pump, I put the truck into First Gear and went backward and scared the two attendants half to death.

According to the Bible, the person who believes in Christ is a new creature. Old things are passed away and all things are become new (2 Corinthians 5:17). When we receive Christ as our Savior, we are given a new nature, a divine nature (2 Peter 1:4). In Ephesians 4:24 Paul uses the expression "the new man." In the same chapter Paul goes on to explain the necessity to put off the "old man" and put on the following four characteristics of the new man.

First, in verse 25, put away lying and speak the truth. Next, in verse 28, steal no more and work with your hands. And then, in verse 29, speak only words that minister grace to the listener. Finally, in verses 31–32, put away bitterness and forgive one another.

As long as I kept using the old gears on my car in place of the new gears on the truck, I kept going backward. Likewise, as long as the "gears" of our Christian life are the same as the "gears" of our old nature, there will be no progress in our life of faith. We'll just keep going backward. Therefore, let's learn the new "gears" of truth, good work, good communication, and forgiveness as soon as possible.

Ken Board

THE TIMER I COULDN'T HEAR

The dentist said to me, "The condition of your gums is not good. If you don't treat the condition, you are going to need oral surgery." I didn't want surgery, so I followed the dentist's advice and bought some mouthwash and began using it twice a day. The dentist told me to put the mouthwash in my mouth and swish it around a little while and then hold it in my mouth for one minute.

I went to the 100-yen shop and bought a small timer. The first time I used the timer I set it for one minute and went into another room to do something while waiting for the timer to ring. I listened carefully for the ring of the timer, but no matter how long I waited, I didn't hear anything, so I went to check on it. The timer was ringing, but the sound was so low that I had to put my ear right beside the timer in order to hear it. I thought, "What good is a timer that I can't hear? When I set the timer, I want the sound to be loud enough for me to hear it anywhere in the house."

The function of a timer is to ring loud enough to be heard. Likewise, the function of a Christian is to witness to the people around him in an audible voice. In Psalm 107:2 the Bible says, "Let the redeemed of the Lord say so." Having been saved from our sins and a meaningless life by the grace of God, instead of being ashamed of our faith, we ought to proclaim it boldly. Through audible words and visible actions we have a responsibility to share our faith with others.

The Christian who will not do that is no different than a timer that can't be heard.

"TOOT, TOOT, TOOT."

When we visited a pastor and his family in Toyohashi, we took some gifts for his wife and his eighteen-month-old son. His wife is from our area, so we thought she would enjoy some special cakes made in our hometown, and we took a set of five plastic musical instruments for the son. He enjoyed playing with four of the instruments, but he had a difficult time with one of them. No matter how hard he tried, he just couldn't blow the trumpet.

Both his father and his mother took turns showing him how to make sound come out of the trumpet, but he was just too small to play it. It took him no time at all, however, to mimic the action of his parents. He held the trumpet close to his mouth and walked around making a "toot, toot, toot" sound with his mouth. The cuteness of his action delighted us all.

The little boy reminded me of some people I have known. They come to church and see the conduct of Christians and mimic them. They sing the same songs, pray the same kind of prayers, and try to live the same kind of life, but they know nothing about being born again by faith in Jesus Christ. Paul's Second Epistle to Timothy prophesied the rise of these people with these words" "having a form of godliness, but denying the power thereof."

This prophecy has become a reality in our generation. Therefore, it would behoove each one of us to pay heed to the exhortation in 2 Corinthians 13:5. "Examine yourselves, whether ye be in the faith; prove your own selves." Is the sound coming out of our Christian life the true sound of a trumpet or our own "toot, toot, toot"?

Ken Board

THE ICING ON THE CAKE

One of the main reasons that people give for changing churches is, "I don't receive a blessing from the pastor's sermons anymore." Whenever I hear these words, I always want to ask this question, "Where did you get the idea that you are supposed to be blessed by the pastor's sermon?" After all, there's not one passage in the Bible that teaches that the purpose of the pastor's sermon is to bless the congregation. There are several passages that reveal the true purpose of the pastor's sermon.

The pastor should use the Word of God as a lamp to lighten the path of his people (Psalm 119:105).

The pastor should use the Word of God as a fire to melt the cold hearts of his people (Jeremiah 23:29).

The pastor should use the Word of God as water to cleanse the impure hearts of his people (Ephesians 5:26).

The pastor should use the Word of God as a sword to cut the deeds of the flesh out of the daily lives of his people (Hebrews 4:12).

The pastor should use the Word of God as a seed to produce the fruit of the Holy Spirit in the hearts of his people (1 Peter 1:23).

The pastor should use the Word of God as milk to help his people grow spiritually (1 Peter 2:2).

In his second epistle to the young evangelist, Timothy, Paul explained the responsibility of a pastor with these words. "Preach the word; be instant in season, out of season; reprove, rebuke, exhort with all longsuffering and doctrine" (4:2). When the sermon of the pastor has accomplished all of these purposes, if in addition to those things the members of his church receive a blessing, well, that's the icing on the cake.

THE BLOODY HAND

I went out to distribute some church flyers, but to be honest, I really didn't want to go. I had been quite busy all morning, so I was tired, but I decided to pass out at least a hundred. After I had placed about seventy of the flyers in mailboxes (legal in Japan), my feet were becoming painful, so I felt even more like quitting for that day.

Just then I looked at the back of my hand and saw that it was bleeding. I must have cut it on one of the mailboxes. I quickly took out my handkerchief and wiped off the blood. There were still thirty flyers left, but in my heart I cried out, "That's it! I am tired. My feet hurt. And now my hand is bleeding. That's it! I quit!"

However, as I stood there and looked at my bleeding hand, I remembered one other bloody hand. It was the hand of the crucified Christ. When the Roman soldiers placed His hands on the cross and drove the nails into them, I can not imagine how great His pain was. When they lifted that cross, the blood from the holy hands of Christ began to fall, drop by drop, to the ground.

According to Matthew 27:29, the soldiers made a crown of thorns and placed it on His head, so there was blood flowing from His head too. Also, in John 19:1 it is written, "Then Pilate therefore took Jesus, and scourged him," so there was blood flowing from His back too. Furthermore, according to John 19:34, one of the soldiers pierced His side with a spear, so there was blood flowing from His side too. Of course, along with His hands, His feet too were nailed to the cross, so there was also blood flowing from His feet.

The Lord Jesus shed His blood to save us from our sins. In order to give us eternal life, He "became obedient unto death, even the death of the cross" (Philippians 2:8). The bloody image of the Savior who died in our place is an image that we should constantly remember.

When we meet various trials and want to quit, once again let us open the Gospels and see the bloody image of the Lord Jesus.

(In case you are wondering, yes, I finished passing out the flyers.)

Ken Board

I LOST $1,000,000 TODAY

I am an avid college basketball fan, so I woke up this morning with a sense of excitement and expectation. It's the first day of "March Madness," the NCAA basketball tournament. However, it wasn't just the tournament that produced the excitement. There is a prediction contest that offers $1,000,000 to any person who can correctly predict the winners of all sixty-three games of the tournament. (This contest is a free contest, so there is no gambling involved.)

This contest is the reason I follow the scores of all of the college basketball games during the year. I want to win the $1,000,000 prize and use the money to buy property and build a beautiful church in Japan. I carefully looked at all of the matchups, the statistics, and the information that I had gathered from the previous November, and with overwhelming confidence predicted the winners of the sixty-three games.

It's now early evening and I am down in the dumps. In one of the games played this afternoon there was an upset, and the team that was upset was one of the winners I had selected. Yes, I lost $1,000,000 today!

Three weeks later: "March Madness" is over and the contest results are not good. I was able to predict accurately the winners of only forty-four of the sixty-three games. Millions of fans participated in the contest, but not one of them was able to predict all sixty-three winners. In fact, the person who won the contest was able to predict only fifty-seven of the sixty-three games accurately.

Just as there wasn't even one person who could record a perfect score in the contest, according to the Bible, there is not even one person who can live a perfect life. There are three passages in the Epistle to the Romans that make this fact clear. "There is none righteous, no, not one" (3:10). "For all have sinned, and come short of the glory of God" (3:23). "All have sinned" (5:12).

Thus far there has been only one individual who has been able to live a perfect life. That one individual is the Lord Jesus Christ, the Son of God who was sent to save us from our sins. "And ye know that he was manifested to take away our sins; and in him is no sin" (1 John 3:5). According to Hebrews 4:15, the Lord Jesus is "without sin." Therefore, the Bible declares that it is Christ and Christ alone who is qualified to be the Savior of the world. (Acts 4:12)

THREE YOUNG LADIES
WHO WOULDN'T BELIEVE ME

Three young ladies attended the wedding of one of their friends in Yokohama. After the wedding they asked me, "What time is tomorrow's service?" I was there as a guest speaker, so I didn't know either. I asked a member of the church staff, and he told me that because tomorrow's service was a special service, it would begin at ten-thirty.

When I relayed this information to the three young ladies, they wouldn't believe me. They had a habit of being late for church, so they thought I was deliberately telling them that the eleven o'clock service was going to start at ten-thirty so they wouldn't show up late. I tried to convince them that I was telling them the truth, but as they left the church to go to their hotel, their faces were still filled with doubt.

The next morning when the pastor sent a church member to pick me up at the hotel, I remarked, "Church starts at ten thirty today, doesn't it?"

He replied, "Oh no, it starts at the regular time, eleven o'clock." When I told him that I had heard that it would start at ten thirty today, he stated, "No, it starts at eleven o'clock."

About 10:20 the three young ladies from my church came running up the street from the subway station in order to be on time for the 10:30 service. I met them in the lobby and tried my best to explain what had happened, but they turned a deaf ear to my explanation.. To this day they think I told them the wrong time so they wouldn't be late for church.

I have a habit of joking with my church members, but this habit produced unbelief in the hearts of those three ladies. It is appropriate actions that make our words believable to other people. In verses 33–37 of the fifth chapter of Matthew, the Lord Jesus explained the relationship between actions and words. He spoke of certain people who had to swear by various things to convince people to believe their words because normally their actions and their words did not agree. In verse 37 the Lord stated, "But let your communication be, Yea, yea; Nay, nay."

If we want others to believe our "yea" or our "nay" or our "the service starts at 10:30," it is necessary that our walk be worthy of our talk.

Ken Board

IT MADE THE
CHURCH LADIES SCREAM

When we decided to move the bookcase at the church, something happened that made me laugh out loud. When we moved the bookcase away from the wall, I noticed a small lizard on the wall. The church ladies are always calm and composed, but when they saw that lizard, every one of them ran screaming into the next room.

I knocked the lizard off the wall into the plastic bag in the trash can, closed the bag, and headed outside. In order to go outside, I had to pass through the room into which the ladies had escaped. When they saw the plastic bag with the lizard inside enter the room, they screamed even louder and tried to hide in the corners of the room. Chuckling, I carried the bag outside, opened it, and let the lizard go.

The church ladies were afraid of the lizard, but the Bible commends the lizard. In Proverbs 30:24 it is written, "There be four things which are little upon the earth, but they are exceeding wise." One of those four things is the lizard. In Proverbs 30:28 we read, "The spider taketh hold with her hands, and is in kings' palaces." (The English Bible uses the word *spider*, but according to Strong's Concordance, the word translated "spider" can also mean "lizard." It is "lizard" in the Japanese Bible.)

The lizard teaches us the value of persistence. It was a simple thing to pick up the lizard and carry it outside, but a lizard doesn't give up so easily. I wouldn't be surprised to see that same lizard back in the church again. Any day now I expect to hear the screams of the church ladies again.

Let's learn from the persistence of the lizard and be diligent in the work of the Lord even though there may be various obstacles. If the lizard can make it into the palace of the king, we should be able to accomplish even tasks that seem impossible, so in spite of the circumstances, let's be diligent in our work for the Lord.

MICHAEL, ROW THE BOAT ASHORE

In both England and in America in the 1960s there was a popular folk song entitled "Michael, Row the Boat Ashore." My good missionary friend's first name is Michael, so whenever I answer a call from him, instead of saying hello, I begin singing "Michael, Row the Boat Ashore."

The other day when I called Mike, he was out, so I left a message for him to call me back. About five minutes later the phone rang. I assumed it was Mike calling me back, so I picked up the phone and started singing, "Michael, Row the Boat Ashore."

Suddenly, I heard the voice of a Japanese man saying, *"Moshi, moshi"* ("hello" in Japanese). When I heard his voice, for a few seconds I couldn't say anything, but finally I replied, "Hello. This is Ken Board."

I recognized the voice as the voice of a pastor of a fairly large church in the Tokyo area. I stuttered and tried my best to explain to him why I answered the phone by singing that song, but I felt extremely embarrassed.

Through this event I learned anew the danger of assumption. People assume that tomorrow they will be alive just as they are today, but the Bible teaches, "Go to now, ye that say, To day or to morrow we will go into such a city, and continue there a year, and buy and sell, and get gain. Whereas ye know not what shall be on the morrow. For what is your life? It is even a vapour, that appeareth for a little time, and then vanisheth away. For that ye ought to say, If the Lord will, we shall live, and do this, or that" (James 4:13–15).

Whether it is a simple thing like a phone call from my friend Michael, or whether it is an important matter concerning life itself, let's be careful of assumptions that can lead to embarrassing or fearful experiences.

Ken Board

"YOU HAVEN'T PRAYED FOR MY TURTLE YET!"

Have you ever prayed for a turtle? I hadn't either until the other day. A Christian family from America moved into the area. Since they do not speak Japanese yet, they began attending our English service on Monday evening.

One Monday their five-year-old son came up to me before the service and asked, "Pastor, would you please pray for my turtle?" When I asked him what he meant, he explained that he had bought a turtle and put it into a box, but the turtle had escaped and he had not been able to find it. "In the service tonight, please pray that I will be able to find my turtle."

I promised him that I would pray for the turtle, but once the service began, I forgot all about it. After the message, I announced, "Let's stand and sing the final hymn." Suddenly, the son shouted, "You haven't prayed for my turtle yet!" After the hymn I prayed for his turtle in the closing prayer.

I wonder if more of our lost friends would be saved if we prayed as zealously for their salvation as that young boy prayed for his lost turtle. We relate our burden for lost friends to others, but there are times when we do not pray for the salvation of those friends even one time during the day. Our example in this matter is the apostle Paul. "Brethren, my heart's desire and prayer to God for Israel is that they might be saved" (Romans 10:1).

If we have family members or friends who are unsaved, let's pray for them the way a five-year-old boy prayed for his turtle.

(By the way, the son found his turtle two days later.)

THE LADY WHO LIVES
IN MY ALARM CLOCK

There is a lady who lives inside my alarm clock. When I push the button on top of the clock, she tells me the time. For example, if it is 2:53 in the afternoon, when I push the button she says, "The time is 2:53 in the afternoon." But that's not all. If I push the button twice, she tells me the date and the temperature. For example, she will say, "Today is Tuesday April the tenth. The temperature is 23 degrees." (Celsius)

She is very helpful, but every now and then she and I have an argument, especially when I can't sleep very well and wake up every thirty–forty minutes. I push the button and she says, "The time is now 2:30 a.m."

I complain to her, "That can't be right. The last time I pushed the button, you said it was two o'clock. Are you trying to tell me I slept only thirty minutes? You must be wrong." However, no matter how many times I press the button, her words never change. "The time is now 2:30."

Just as there is a lady who lives inside my clock, according to the Bible, God the Holy Spirit dwells within every Christian (1 Corinthians 6:19). The various things that the Holy Spirit does for the believer are explained in the eighth chapter of Romans. One of those things is guidance (Romans 8:14). When it seems the believer is about to lose his way and can't decide which path to take, the Holy Spirit guides him.

The regretful thing is that, just as I complain to the lady who lives inside my clock, there are times when believers complain to the Holy Spirit and rebel against His leadership. But just as the lady in my clock always tells me the right time, the Holy Spirit will always lead us to the right path, so let's follow His leadership obediently.

Ken Board

THE FRIED OCTOPUS PARTY

L ast week a church celebrated its second anniversary. The missionary who started the church was in the States, so I conducted the anniversary service. The previous week the church members had decided that they wanted to celebrate the anniversary with a fried octopus party after church.

Speaking honestly, I don't care much for fried octopus. I have eaten it several times, but not one time have I ever thought it was delicious. I have never ordered it at a restaurant. However, the fried octopus that the church ladies fixed that night was unlike any other fried octopus I had ever seen—because there was no octopus in it!

One of the ladies explained that when her children were small, they had a hard time chewing fried octopus, so she began making it with shrimp, cuttlefish, and cheese instead of octopus. As I prepared to eat fried octopus with no octopus in it, I was thinking, "I wonder what fried octopus with no octopus in it tastes like? I wonder if it is delicious?"

I put the first one into my mouth. It was great! Later when someone told me to put a little mayonnaise on top, it was even more delicious. I ended up eating several of them. Later on I just had to ask the lady, "Even though there is no octopus in it, do you still call this dish fried octopus at your home?" She replied that they did.

When I ate the fried octopus with no octopus in it, I was reminded of sermons that I hear or read now and then. The men who wrote or preached those messages thought they were preaching the gospel, but their gospel was a gospel that had no gospel in it.

According to the Bible in 1 Corinthians 15:1–5, the "gospel" is the following three things: First, Jesus died for our sins. Second, Jesus was buried. Third, Jesus rose again the third day. Any "gospel" that leaves out even one of these three truths is not the true gospel. It's like fried octopus with no octopus in it. It may be a tasty message, but it's different from the gospel declared in the Bible.

NO COLD WATER

Last week we held the final service at the old location. In the afternoon we loaded into our vans the pulpit, chairs, tables, and other items that had not yet been moved to the new location. It was extremely hot, so my mouth became parched. Thinking, "I'd love to have some cold water," I suddenly remembered something that made me very happy. There was cold water in the refrigerator at the new church!

Looking forward to that cold water, I jumped into the van and headed for the new location. When we arrived at church, I hurried inside, opened the refrigerator, poured some of the delicious-looking water into a cup, and drank it. In the next instant I was greatly disappointed. The water wasn't cold at all. I felt like spitting the warm water out of my mouth.

I wondered out loud, "Is the refrigerator broken?"

One of the church ladies replied, "Pastor, don't you remember? We turned off the power when we left the other day."

I remembered. "Oh yeah, last Thursday when we moved the heavy items here, before we left, I turned the power off." I myself was the cause of my disappointment.

When we moved to the new location, we prayed that many people whose souls are thirsty will come seeking Jesus Christ who is the Water of Life. However, just as I was disappointed because there was no cold water, if there is no spiritual power in our church, many thirsty souls who visit our church may leave greatly disappointed. On the other hand, if the power of the Holy Spirit is overflowing in us, we can expect the same thing that took place in Acts 4:31–33 to take place at our church: "They were all filled with the Holy Ghost, and they spake the word of God with boldness . . . And with great power gave the apostles witness of the resurrection of the Lord Jesus."

Ken Board

THE "SA, SHI, SU, SE, SO" OF JAPANESE COOKING

Every other Saturday I attend a ladies' meeting at a nearby church, First, the pastor teaches a Bible lesson and then I teach English to the ladies. In the introduction of his latest lesson, the pastor mentioned "the sa, shi, su, se, so of Japanese cooking," which I found quite interesting.

Cooks in Japan are diligent to use the following five ingredients in their cooking:

SA is *satoo* (sugar).

SHI is *shio* (salt).

SU is *su* (vinegar).

SE is *shoyuu* (soy sauce; used to be called *seuyuu* but is now called *shoyuu*).

SO is *miso* (bean paste).

Using the same five letters of the Japanese alphabet, we can make a recipe for a joyful, victorious Christian life that is pleasing to the Lord (emphasis mine, in the following verses).

SA = sacrifice. "Present your bodies a living *sacrifice*, holy acceptable unto God" (Romans 12:1). "Let us offer the *sacrifice* of praise to God continually" (Hebrews 13:15).

SHI = shine. "Let your light so *shine* before men, that they may see your good works, and glorify your Father which is in heaven" (Matthew 5:16). "Do all things without murmuring and disputing: That ye may be blameless and harmless, the sons of God, without rebuke, in the midst of a crooked and perverse nation, among whom ye *shine* as lights in the world" (Philippians 2:14–15).

SU = supplication. "Praying always with all prayer and *supplication* in the Spirit, and watching thereunto with all perseverance and *supplication* for all saints" (Ephesians 6:18). "Be careful for nothing; but in everything by prayer and *supplication* with thanksgiving let your requests be made known unto God" (Philippians 4:6).

SE = serve. "*Serve* the Lord with gladness" (Psalm 100:2). "By love *serve* one another" (Galatians 5:13).

SO = sober. "Therefore, let us not sleep, as do others; but let us watch and be *sober*" (1 Thessalonians 5:6). "But the end of all things is at hand: be ye therefore *sober*, and watch unto prayer" (1 Peter 4:7).

Whether it is our relationship with the Lord or our relationship with other people, if we will mix these five spiritual "ingredients" into our daily life, we shall be able to enjoy a much more "delicious" Christian life.

Ken Board

WHY DO I KEEP
LOWERING THE WINDOW?

This year I had an ETC (electronic toll collection) device installed in my car. It's a very convenient device. When I approach the expressway tollgate, I can pass through without stopping; plus, I don't have to wait in long lines to pay the toll, so ETC is like a delightful toy to me.

When I had the device installed, the Kyushu Expressway was already receiving payments by ETC, but the Kitakyushu City Expressway hadn't installed the necessary equipment yet, so whenever I traveled that road, I had to stop my car, lower the window, and pay the toll just as I had always done. Finally, this month the Kitakyushu City Expressway too began accepting ETC payments; however, because I was so accustomed to lowering the car window whenever I approached the tollgate, even after I was able to begin going through the ETC gate, I would always lower the window. One day I realized what I was doing and asked myself, "Why do you keep lowering the window?" It took a while, but finally I was able to break the habit.

It's quite difficult to stop an action that has become a habit of our daily life. Proverbs explains this difficulty with these descriptive words: "Though thou shouldest bray a fool in a mortar among wheat with a pestle, yet will not his foolishness depart from him." (27:22).

It is also difficult to cease the bad habits of our Christian life. In Jeremiah 13:23 the Lord said to Jeremiah, "Can the Ethiopian change his skin, or the leopard his spots? Then may ye also do good, that are accustomed to do evil." Even Christians can become accustomed to a habit that is not pleasing to the Lord.

The Bible calls these habits to which we become accustomed "the sin which doth so easily beset us" and exhorts us to lay aside those habits (Hebrews 12:1). Of course, the leopard can't change its spots, but the leopard doesn't have the power of the Lord to help him as a Christian does, so we should be able to overcome the habits in our life which do not please the Lord.

ONE MOMENT OF CARELESSNESS

It was just one brief moment of carelessness. We returned home from church one cold evening and I parked the car in the driveway. Our driveway is on a slope, so I have to make certain I set the emergency brake before I get out of the car. However, this night I was tired both physically and mentally; plus, I was in a hurry to be inside our warm house, so I failed to set the emergency brake. The instant I took my foot off the brake and stepped out of the car, it began rolling backward. I jumped back into the car and pulled the emergency brake, but before I could stop the car, the open door collided with the drainpipe coming down from the roof.

The door was bent so badly that I couldn't get it shut. I closed it as much as possible, and my wife helped me wire it in place. However, because of that one moment of carelessness, for one month I couldn't get out of the car on the driver's side. I had to crawl across the car and exit on the passenger side. Not only that, when I finally had enough money to have the door repaired, it cost me $400. All for one moment of carelessness.

One of the dangers in trying to live a life that is pleasing to the Lord is that one moment of carelessness. We can see it in the lives of many of the characters of the Bible. In one moment of carelessness Abraham lied to the king of Egypt (Genesis 12). In one moment of carelessness Samson lost his power (Judges 16). In one moment of carelessness David committed a terrible sin (2 Samuel 11).

As we read the records of these men of great faith who fell into the Devil's trap in one moment of carelessness, let's be on guard and pay attention to the solemn warning of Christ. "Watch and pray, that ye enter not into temptation: the spirit indeed is willing, but the flesh is weak" (Matthew 26:41).

Ken Board

THE BANK ALARM BUTTON

My latest visit to the bank was quite exciting. I inserted my bank card into the ATM machine, put in my PIN number, indicated the amount of cash I wanted, and waited. Suddenly, the words "Out of Order" appeared on the screen and the ATM came to a halt with my bank card and my money still inside.

There was a phone nearby for people who need assistance, so I picked up the phone and explained my dilemma to a bank teller who told me to push the "call button." I looked around and saw a button below the telephone and pushed it. Guess what? It wasn't the "call button." It was the "crime prevention" alarm button.

Instantly, several loud bells began ringing. My first impulse was to escape as quickly as I could, but my bank card and money were still inside the ATM machine. Shortly, a bank employee came running out and pushed the button and the bells ceased to ring. It was just another chapter in my long story of embarrassing experiences.

According to the Bible, there is a "sin prevention" alarm button like that crime prevention alarm button dwelling in every Christian. In John 14:17 the Lord Jesus stated, "Even the Spirit of truth; whom the world cannot receive, because it seeth him not, neither knoweth him: but ye know him, for he dwelleth with you, and shall be in you." Also, in 1 Corinthians 3:16 it is written, "Know ye not that ye are the temple of God, and that the Spirit of God dwelleth in you?" Verse nineteen of chapter six of the same letter teaches us that "your body is the temple of the Holy Ghost which is in you."

Whenever a Christian sins, immediately an alarm bell begins to echo in his heart. That "alarm bell" is the voice of the Holy Spirit saying, "What you just did was a sin." In fact, even before we commit a sin, the alarm bell in our heart starts ringing, "What you are about to do is not right."

When the "alarm bell" of our heart begins ringing, there is only one way to turn it off. We must confess our sins to the Lord, repent of them, and ask God to forgive us.

THE PICKLE JAR LID

While my cheeseburger was frying, I took the mayonnaise and the pickles out of the refrigerator and put a generous serving of both on my bread. The cheeseburger wasn't quite done yet, so I decided to go ahead and put the lid back on the pickle jar and return it to the refrigerator, but the lid wouldn't fit. I thought maybe I was trying to put it on the wrong way, so I tried again, but it still wouldn't fit. When I tried for the third time and it still wouldn't fit, I became frustrated.

In an angry voice I shouted, "I took this lid off this jar just two or three minutes ago. Why won't it fit?" Just then I looked at the lid carefully and realized why it wouldn't fit. I was trying to put the mayonnaise jar lid on the pickle jar. I could have stood there all day and tried to put the mayonnaise jar lid on the pickle jar, but it would not have worked no matter how hard I tried.

It is the same with the church. According to the Bible, the Lord Jesus is the head of the church (Ephesians 5:23). Therefore, when we try to lift up someone other than Christ as the head of the church—for example, a pastor or a church officer or a bishop or an organization—the image of that church will be different from the image of the church that can be seen in the Bible. Not only that, it will be difficult for that church to carry out its most important mission—namely, world evangelization. It's like trying to put the mayonnaise jar lid on the pickle jar.

According to Ephesians 1:20–22, God "raised Christ from the dead, and set him at his own right hand in the heavenly places, Far above all principality, and power, and might, and dominion, and every name that is named, not only in this world, but also in that which is to come, And hath put all things under his feet, and gave him to be the head over all things to the church."

Ken Board

THE REAL ME

I received a notice from the police department that my driver's license had been suspended, so in order to have my license renewed, I went to the driver's examination office to take a test. First, they had me take a "personality test." I answered the questions honestly with confidence. However, when I saw the results, I was dismayed. These were the three comments listed on my test results:

You have a tendency to think only about your own driving and ignore the position of the other person.

When driving, your frame of mind is not on obeying traffic laws and safe driving procedures.

You are an impatient, restless driver.

When I read these results, I thought, "These things might be true of me when I am driving, but it's just when I'm driving. The *real* me is different." However, in the next instant the police officer said, "A person's driving reveals his real character." Then he instructed me to look at page fifteen in the driver's manual. There, among all the Japanese words, was one sentence in English: "A man drives as he lives."

To be honest, his words cut through my heart like a sharp knife. Immediately, I sensed a need to take an honest look at myself. "Selfish, disobedient, impatient, restless"—is this the real me? If so, I knew it would be necessary for me to repent before the Lord.

Just as my style of driving revealed my true character, in the Christian life it is adversity that reveals the reality of our faith. In the parable of the sower, the Lord Jesus said, "And these are they likewise which are sown on stony ground; who, when they have heard the word, immediately receive it with gladness; And have no root in themselves, and so endure but for a time: afterward, when affliction or persecution ariseth for the word's sake, immediately they are offended" (Mark 4:16–17).

Is our faith the same when there is affliction and when there is no affliction, or is it different? If it is different, which is our real faith?

THE WHITE SNAKE

When we took our children to the amusement park in Beppu, we found a small zoo inside the park. It cost extra to enter the zoo, but we decided to pay the money and check it out. I was surprised to find a small shrine inside the zoo. I wondered, "What is a shrine doing in the zoo?" I entered the small building and looked to the right and saw nothing, but when I looked to the left, I was startled to see a *kamidana* (a small shelf upon which a "god" is placed). Wondering what "god" was being worshipped at this shrine, I walked closer and saw a white snake. It was alive.

Just then the caretaker of the shrine entered, saw me, and asked, "Would you like to hold the snake in your hands?" I started to refuse but had a quick change of heart and replied, "Yes, I would."

The caretaker removed the snake from the altar and placed it in my hands. I held "god" in my hands. Suddenly, the snake began crawling up my arm toward my face, so I decided that was enough fellowship with "god" for one day.

To this day, that white snake is the most unusual thing I have seen in Japan. I left that shrine with a heart filled with thanksgiving. I was thankful that I believe not in a "god" that I can hold in my hands but a God who holds me in His hands. In John 10:27–29 Christ said, "My sheep hear my voice, and I know them, and they follow me: And I give unto them eternal life; and they shall never perish, neither shall any man pluck them out of my hand. My Father, which gave them me, is greater than all; and no man is able to pluck them out of my Father's hand."

Today and every day let's be thankful for the protection of the God who holds us in His hands. "My soul followeth hard after thee: thy right hand upholdeth me" (Psalm 63:8).

Ken Board

A SLIPPER FULL OF YOGURT

I always have yogurt for breakfast. Most of the yogurt at the grocery store comes in small cartons and has sugar in it, so I buy the large cartons of plain yogurt, put about half of the carton into a big bowl, and add some sweetener. I usually read the newspaper while I'm having breakfast. As I read the paper, I hold the bowl with the yogurt in my left hand and a spoon in my right hand and eat while I read. When I am ready to turn the page, I set the bowl of yogurt down on the table.

However, one morning when I put the bowl of yogurt down in order to turn the newspaper, I missed the table and the bowl full of yogurt landed upside down on my foot. There was yogurt on my foot, yogurt on the floor, and my slipper was full of yogurt. I was quite upset at my carelessness. It took quite a while to clean up the mess. That day I learned that when you set down a bowl of yogurt, if you don't have something to set it on, you will regret it.

Life is the same. If we do not have some sort of support for our life, sooner or later we shall come to regret it. The problem is finding the proper support. If we make money or things or the job or another person our support, through sudden events such as accidents or natural disasters or the circumstances of society, our support falls and our life becomes a mess.

In Psalm 18 David recorded the painful circumstances of his life with these words: "The sorrows of death compassed me about: and the floods of ungodly men made me afraid. The sorrows of hell compassed me about: the snares of death prevented me" (verses 4–5).

Placed in these circumstances, what did David do? "In my distress I called upon the Lord, and cried unto my God" (verse 6). When David did that, what happened?

"The Lord was my stay. He brought me forth also into a large place; he delivered me" (verses 18–19).

When our life ends up like a slipper full of yogurt, let's call upon the name of the Lord. He is the only reliable support.

THE UPSIDE-DOWN RAZOR BLADE

When I was young, I shaved every day, but now my beard doesn't grow as quickly, so I shave only two or three times a week. Thus, I can use the same razor blade for quite a while.

The other day when I put a new blade in my razor and began to shave, I was surprised. I exclaimed, "What a smooth blade! I've never used a blade this smooth. I can't even feel it cutting." But when I touched my face, I was amazed to discover that my beard had not been shaved at all. I looked at the razor blade. When I inserted the blade into the razor, I had put it in upside down. That's why it felt so smooth. When I reinserted the blade and began to shave again, it still felt smooth, but I could sense the beard being shaved. When the blade was inserted properly, I could feel the effect of the blade on my face.

It's the same when we read the Word of God. If our heart attitude is correct, the Word of God will have the same effect on our hearts that the razor blade has on our faces. "For the word of God is quick, and powerful, and sharper than any two-edged sword, piercing even to the dividing asunder of soul and spirit, and of the joints and marrow, and is a discerner of the thoughts and intents of the heart" (Hebrews 4:12).

When we insert the Word of God into our hearts, if there are in our hearts preconceived ideas, opinions, and prejudices to which we give priority, the power of the Word of God to cut harmful practices and thoughts out of our faith life will be hindered. Therefore, when we read the Bible, first let's cast out of our hearts anything that might interfere with the effect of the Word of God and give priority to the Word and incline our hearts toward obeying it. "I have inclined my heart to perform thy statutes always, even unto the end" (Psalm 119:112).

Ken Board

THE CRISPY CREAM PUFFS

L ast week I had supper at the home of some missionary friends. Even though they are Americans, I wanted to observe the Japanese custom of taking a gift. At the shopping center I saw a store selling crispy cream puffs. I had probably passed by that store hundreds of times but had never bought anything there, but this time I passed by just as I was wondering what to take to take to my friends, so I decided to take them some cream puffs. As I waited for the cream puffs, I was surprised at two things.

First, the store does not put the cream into the puff until after a customer places an order, for if the cream is put into ahead of time, the puff loses its crispiness.

Second, after putting the cream into the puffs, the lady placed each cream puff on a scale and weighed it. In order to satisfy the customer, the store checks to make certain there is plenty of cream in the puff. In my mind I gave that store a high rating.

The Bible compares a righteous way of living to a just scale. "Ye shall do no unrighteousness in judgment, in meteyard, in weight, or in measure. Just balances, just weights, a just ephah, and a just hin, shall ye have" (Leviticus 19:35–36). "A false balance is abomination to the Lord: but a just weight is his delight" (Proverbs 11:1). Just as I rated highly the store that weighed each one of the cream puffs, the Lord will rate highly the Christian who lives a righteous life, and He will be pleased with that Christian. By all means, a Christian should put away words and actions that deceive others and live an honest life. The two characteristics that should stand out in the life of a Christian are honesty and righteousness.

"Let us walk honestly" (Romans 13:13).

I'M BEGINNING
TO GET SUSPICIOUS

L ately, some of the neighborhood children come by the house and invite me and my daughter to go on a walk with them. I assumed they enjoyed going on a walk with me, so I was happy to go with them. However, for a couple of reasons I have become suspicious of the real purpose of the children's invitation to go on a walk with them.

First, no matter which way we go, we always end up going by the candy store. Also, before we leave my house, the children always ask, "Do you have any money with you?" This daily walk with the children has become a financial problem because the number of children has been steadily increasing. Also, at first I was buying them gum, which cost about ten cents, but now I am buying each one of them ice cream that costs about sixty cents.

Do you suppose some of us have the same attitude as the attitude of those children when we go to church? In other words, our reason for going to church is not to have fellowship with the Lord but to receive some sort of blessing from the Lord.

Psalm 100 teaches us the correct mindset for going to church. According to verse 2, our purpose in going to church is not just to meet other Christians but to "serve the Lord with gladness and come before his presence with singing."

Also, according to verse 5, our reason for going to church should not be just to receive a blessing from the Lord but to set our heart on His goodness, His mercy, and His truth. When these two purposes become our real purposes for going to the Lord's house, the blessings we shall receive will be much more wonderful than a temporary blessing such as a "pack of gum" or some "ice cream."

Ken Board

THE STAIN ON MY FINGER

I am upset this morning. The monthly pastors' meeting will begin in about two hours, and I have a black stain on my finger. Yesterday when I changed one of the ink tanks in my printer, I accidentally turned the tank upside down and black ink spilled all over my finger.

I immediately washed my finger with soap, but the stain wouldn't come off. I didn't want to attend tomorrow's pastors' meeting with this stain on my finger, so next I tried using dish soap, but I still couldn't remove the stain. I thought about using laundry detergent, but I was concerned about the damage to my skin.

Now it's the afternoon. I had no choice but to attend the pastors' meeting with the stain on my finger. No one asked, "Pastor Board, what's that stain on your finger?" but I'm sure they were thinking that I had not washed my hands for several days.

My concern for the stain on my finger mirrors the concern of many people for the stain on their heart. It's a stain called "sin." According to the Bible, all people are sinners by nature, and when people become aware of their sins, they try various methods to remove those sins. Some people try a soap called "religion." Others try to remove their sins with a detergent called "self-improvement, while others try a cleanser called "good works."

No matter what "soap" he may choose, it is impossible for man to cleanse his heart that has been defiled by the stain of sin. However, there is one "soap" that will cleanse our hearts whiter than snow. That "soap" is the precious blood of the Lord Jesus Christ who died on the cross for our sins. According to the Bible, if we will admit our sins and believe in the Lord Jesus Christ, "the blood of Jesus Christ cleanses us from all sin" (1 John 1:7).

THE CROOKED HEATING PADS

My shoulder has been hurting lately, so I went to the drugstore and bought some heating pads. Normally, heating pads are divided into two parts. You peel off one side, then peel off the other side and apply it to the painful area; however, the heating pads that I bought were divided into three parts—in other words: left, center, and right.

I thought it was somewhat strange, but I peeled the back off the three sections and tried to apply it to my shoulder. Right away I discovered that it was not going to be a simple thing to do. Before I could apply the heating pad to my shoulder, the right section became stuck to the left section, and no matter how hard I pulled, I could not get them apart, so I threw away the first pad.

Somehow I was finally able to get the next pad on my shoulder, but it wasn't flat and it lay crooked. The next morning was the same. Finally, when I decided to read the instructions, I learned how to put on the pads divided into three sections. First, you peel the back off the middle section and apply it, and then it is a simple thing to apply the right and left sections. Of course, if I had read the instructions before I tried to use the heating pads, I would not have had to throw away the first pad, and the next pads would have been flat and straight.

How similar this is to life itself. If we would start out by reading the Bible—the instruction book for the Christian life—we would know what to do when we meet trials and adversities. However, on many occasions, we don't look for the solutions until we have tried to work out the problems by our own power and wisdom. If we will read the instruction book first, we will know ahead of time how to handle the various difficulties of our Christian life.

"This book of the law shall not depart out of thy mouth; but thou shalt meditate therein day and night, that thou mayest observe to do according to all that is written therein: for then thou shalt make thy way prosperous, and thou shalt have good success" (Joshua 1:8).

Ken Board

"DEAR LORD,
PLEASE HELP THE GIANTS."

The husband of one of the church ladies was seriously ill, and the pastor asked me to pray for him. As I prayed, I was thinking, "Do I want to pray for Brother So-and-So or do I want to pray for Sister So-and-So's husband?" In Japanese "brother" is *kyoodai* and "husband" is *shujin*. In my uncertainty concerning which word to use, I ended up taking the first part of *kyoodai* and the last part of *shujin* and prayed, "Dear Lord, please help the *kyojin*."

When I finished my prayer and looked at the pastor, he was smiling. The word *kyojin* is the Japanese word for the Tokyo Giants pro baseball team. Instead of praying, "Lord, please help Brother So-and-So," or "Lord, please help Sister So-and-So's husband," I had prayed, "Lord, please help the Giants." The pastor of the church is a big fan of the Giants, so he was pleased; however, I don't like the Giants at all, so later I asked the Lord to cancel my prayer. It was the first time since I became a Christian that I asked the Lord to cancel one of my prayers.

Another time when I was praying for a lady during the ladies' meeting, I intended to pray, "Dear Lord, please hold her up," but instead I prayed, "Dear Lord, please hold her down." The ladies had a good chuckle after the prayer.

I don't know if you have ever become confused during a prayer and didn't know exactly what to say, but I have been in that situation several times, especially when I'm praying in Japanese, so I am extremely thankful for the wonderful truth written in Romans 8:26: "For we know not what we should pray as we ought: but the Spirit itself maketh intercession for us with groaning which cannot be uttered."

THE LUCKY PUPPY

There's a very lucky puppy living in the next town. My daughter found this dog at the park and brought him home. He was quite a cute puppy, but I told my daughter to take the puppy right back to the park. My wife and daughter felt sorry for the puppy, however, so they decided that we would keep the puppy until we could find someone to take it.

Our cat was not pleased with this decision. The puppy ate the cat's food, chased the cat, and monopolized my daughter's time.

I also was not pleased with this decision. When I woke up and headed for the bathroom each morning, invariably I would step in a "present" the dog had left on the floor during the night. I don't know how many times I started the day off in a disagreeable mood because of the dog's "presents," and I don't know how many times I told that dog, "You're outta here today!" but my family always stopped me.

My daughter went from house to house in the neighborhood searching for a home for the puppy. She even had one of her friends post a picture of the puppy at the local supermarket.

On the second Saturday of each month there is a place in this city where people who want dogs and people who want to get rid of dogs can meet. We took the puppy to that place and a family living in the next town decided they wanted our puppy.

If my daughter had not found the puppy at the park, he probably would have starved to death. Also, if my wife and daughter had not felt sorry for the puppy and protected him, I probably would have taken him back to the park one of those mornings when I felt his "present" under my foot. Now the puppy is living happily ever after in the next town.

There are people who go through the same experience as that puppy. They have been discarded by their family and friends. They are despised by everyone that knows them. Their very existence is an existence of loneliness and pain. However, according to the Bible, there is a merciful God who loves those people and sent His only Son to die on the cross and save them from their sins and life of misery.

"God commendeth his love toward us, in that, while we were yet sinners, Christ died for us" (Romans 5:8).

THE POLICEMAN'S WATCH

Because there are several schools in the area around the church, every morning from seven o'clock to nine o'clock, except for one road, all roads are blocked, and only vehicles with special permits are allowed to drive on those roads. One morning shortly before nine o'clock, one of our church members was stopped by a policeman. The church member pointed to his watch and stated, "According to my watch, it's past nine o'clock."

The policeman pointed to his watch and replied, "According to my watch, it's not nine o'clock yet."

Which watch do you suppose the policeman believed? Of course, he decided that his own watch was the correct one and warned the church member that he would be fined if he committed the same violation again.

When the pastor of the church points out specific sins in his message, occasionally there are people who protest and say, "In my opinion, that is not a sin." Like the policeman who had to choose between his own watch and the church member's watch, the pastor has to choose between human words and the Word of God. Of course, the faithful pastor will always make the Word of God the standard of human conduct. The Bible is the standard that God has given to the church. When our actions and opinions do not agree with the teachings of the Bible, it is not the Bible that is wrong. We are wrong.

"All scripture is given by inspiration of God, and is profitable for doctrine, for reproof, for correction, for instruction in righteousness: That the man of God may be perfect, throughly furnished unto all good works" (2 Timothy 3:16–17).

FISHING WITH CHEWING GUM

I love fishing, but I may be the world's worst fisherman. The other day when I went fishing with three friends, tiny fish kept stealing the bait from my hook. After this happened several times, I lost my cool. I yelled, "You thieving fish, I have had it with you!"

Just then I thought of a brilliant plan. I took the gum out of my mouth and put it on the hook. I thought, "The next time one of those fish tries to steal my bait, when he bites the bait, he'll get stuck to the gum. He's mine!" However, no matter how many times I threw the hook with the gum attached to it into the water, the fish wouldn't come near it. It was obvious they could tell the difference between real bait and chewing gum.

When we witness to others, let's remember the fish and the chewing gum. No matter how skillfully we may select our words, if our walk is not worthy of our words, people will quickly recognize the discrepancy in our witness. In 1 John 3:18 the Bible says, "My little children, let us not love in word, neither in tongue; but in deed and in truth."

We may be able to present the gospel brilliantly, but if our friends and neighbors are watching our unrighteous deeds, they will not receive our message. Even if we are able to persuade them to go to church with us, when they compare the message of the pastor with our hypocritical way of living, they will come to the conclusion that our faith has no substance other than words. When we try with all our heart to win someone to Christ but are not successful, let's do a little self-examination and check to see if the deeds of our life are contradicting the words of our mouth. If they are, we are fishing with chewing gum.

Ken Board

THE JOY CAFÉ

ear my home there is a restaurant called "Joyful." This restaurant has an all-you-can-drink "drink bar" (no alcoholic beverages) called the Joy Café. When I ate breakfast there with a pastor recently, I noticed the five words that this restaurant uses to advertise the drink bar: happy, enjoy, refresh, relax, and tasty. (Many Japanese signs that include English do not distinguish between adjectives and verbs. Of course, the sign should have read "happy, enjoyable, refreshing, relaxing, and tasty.")

When you think about it, these same five words can describe the qualities of God and His Word.

HAPPY: "He that keepeth the law, happy is he" (Proverbs 29:18).

ENJOYABLE: "Thy words were found, and I did eat them; and thy word was unto me the joy and rejoicing of mine heart" (Jeremiah 15:16).

REFRESHING: "The Lord is my shepherd; I shall not want. He maketh me to lie down in green pastures: he leadeth me beside the still water. He restoreth my soul" (Psalm 23:1–3).

RELAXING: "Great peace have they which love thy law" (Psalm 119:165).

TASTY: "How sweet are thy words unto my taste! Yea, sweeter than honey to my mouth!" (Psalm 119:103).

God's Joy Café is also "all-you-can-drink," so let's drink until our hearts are overflowing with the many blessings that come from the Word of God.

THE INVALID PASSWORD

Wondering if I might have some new e-mail messages, I typed in my password, but the screen responded, "Invalid password." Thinking, "No way my password is invalid," I entered it again and the same message appeared on the screen, so I contacted my provider and received a new password.

For two or three days there were no problems, and then the "invalid password" message showed up again. I contacted the provider again and received a new password. The same "invalid password" message kept popping up every two to three days. Finally, I decided to call the provider in the States and explain the problem to him.

At first even he didn't know what to do, but suddenly he asked me, "Is there someone using your main computer in the States while you are in Japan?"

When I answered, "Yes," he told me, "Whoever is using that computer must be changing the password every few days."

Right away I called the young man living at my house in the States and asked him, "Have you changed the password lately?"

When he told me that he indeed had changed it several times lately, I laughed and explained the situation to him. "When you changed the password, I received an 'invalid password' message, so I changed the password, and you received an 'invalid password' message. We have been changing the password back and forth for the past few weeks." Now we are both using the same password, so the problem has been solved.

I am thankful that the Word of God is not like an e-mail password that suddenly becomes invalid. "Being born again, not of corruptible seed, but of incorruptible, by the word of God, which liveth and abideth for ever. For all flesh is as grass, and all the glory of man as the flower of grass. The grass withereth, and the flower thereof falleth away: But the word of the Lord endureth for ever" (1 Peter 1:23–25).

Christians can read new e-mails from the Lord at any time and we don't even need a password.

Ken Board

I SHOULD HAVE GONE TO HEAVEN
FIVE YEARS AGO

When I went for my bimonthly blood test and ultrasound at the urological clinic, the doctor asked, "How many years has it been?" I replied, "Exactly ten years ago."

(A little over ten years ago I was diagnosed with prostate cancer. Further tests revealed that the cancer had already spread into the bones. In addition to chemotherapy, I participated in an experimental program at a well-known cancer center in the United States. I was told that I probably had five years left at the most.)

The doctor said, "I am amazed. Your PSA is zero. I can no longer see any cancer in the ultrasound pictures." Then he said these wonderful words, "You are almost cured."

I replied, "I am waiting for the day when you tell me that I am cured."

Again he stated, "I am amazed."

I related my testimony to him and tried to have him understand the power of prayer. When my friends and coworkers heard that I had cancer, the phone calls, cards, letters, and e-mails began arriving daily. A number of people even came to visit me. Their messages all said the same thing: "We're praying for you." Probably there were thousands of people around the world praying for me every day.

Like most people in Japan who have no concept of a living God who is concerned with the daily affairs of people, the doctor listened in silence and offered no comment when my testimony had ended.

How is it that Christians can pray with assurance that God will hear and answer their prayers? We believe in the power of prayer because our God is a living God. He is not an idol made of wood or stone or a long-departed ancestor. We pray in the name of the Savior who died on the cross for our sins, was buried, and arose on the third day. We pray in the name of the Lord Jesus Christ who lives evermore. My doctor couldn't understand it, but each and every Christian believes with all of his heart in the words written in Hebrews 7:25: "He is able also to save them to the uttermost that come unto God by him, seeing he ever liveth to make intercession for them."

THE WRONG CAT

During the New Year holidays my wife and I worked on a jigsaw puzzle. It was a beautiful scene of an old Japanese-style house and garden with Mount Fuji in the background, but it was one of the most difficult puzzles we have ever tried to put together. We had completed about one-third of the puzzle when our cat, Button, jumped up on the table and knocked several pieces to the floor.

It angered me to see a lot of our hard work ruined, so I grabbed a newspaper and took off after Button. I chased her around and around the house until I finally cornered her. I raised the newspaper to smack her when I noticed that it wasn't Button. It was another cat, Curly, that was staying with us at the time. Somewhere during the chase Button escaped and Curly became my target. It would have been an injustice if Curly had been punished for Button's actions.

There is a lot of injustice in the world. There are occasions when innocent people are found guilty and punished. There are also situations like the one with Button and Curly where the true culprit escapes punishment. However, when each one of us stands before the Lord, the judgment of the Lord will be a just and righteous judgment. We may have taken the blame for someone else's sin here on the earth, but according to Romans 14:12, "Every one of us shall give account of himself to God."

The Bible also declares, "The judgments of the Lord are true and altogether righteous" (Psalm 19:9). Therefore, when we stand before the Lord, let's stand before him not as a guilty Button but as an innocent Curly.

Ken Board

THE ROARING WIND

For a few weeks there had been a ringing in my ears, so I finally went to the doctor. He used a special machine to test my hearing. It was a rather simple test. I went into a soundproof room, put on headphones, and pushed a button as soon as I could hear the sound coming through the headphones.

Two weeks later I went back to the doctor for another exam, but this time it wasn't so easy, for in addition to the sound I was trying to hear, there was also the sound of blowing wind. After a while the sound of the wind changed to a roaring sound. I had to concentrate extremely hard to hear the sound I was trying to hear, so it was quite a difficult exam.

As I was leaving the doctor's office, I remembered a passage in the fourteenth chapter of Matthew. One night the disciples of the Lord Jesus were on a ship in the midst of the sea when the wind suddenly picked up and the ship began to be tossed about by the waves. All of a sudden, along with the sound of the roaring of the wind and the sound of the waves crashing into the ship, the disciples heard the voice of the Lord Jesus. "Be of good cheer; it is I; be not afraid" (Matthew 14:27).

Under normal conditions it is easy for us to hear the voice of the Lord Jesus; however, when the storms come, and the winds began to blow, and the waves of adversity began crashing into our life, hearing the voice of the Lord may become quite difficult. With a heart full of fear, we cry out, "Lord, where are you? Lord, this is a terrible storm. Why don't you help me?" However, if we will listen carefully, we too will hear the Lord saying to us, "Be of good cheer; it is I; be not afraid."

"The floods have lifted up, O Lord, the floods have lifted up their voice; the floods lift up their waves. The Lord on high is mightier than the noise of many waters, yea, than the mighty waves of the sea" (Psalm 93:3–4).

MY CHANCE TO SIT
IN THE SUPER BOX

I shouted with excitement, "Yes, yes! I want them!" A representative from a company with which I do business had just called me to offer me two tickets in the "Super Box" that the company rents at Yahoo Dome. The Super Box seats are the best seats in the stadium and quite expensive. Almost every time I go to see the Hawks play, I look up at the Super Box seats and think, "Just once. Just one time I would like to watch a game from the Super Box." Therefore, when I received the call saying that there were two seats available for free, I shouted my reply, "Yes, yes! I want them!"

The company representative explained, "You have to write the names of the people who will use the seats, and you have to order your meal ahead of time, so I will send you a document by fax. Fill in the document and return it to me by fax."

When the fax arrived, I was waiting with my pen in my hand. However, when I saw the date of the game, my overflowing joy changed to deep sadness. A pastor friend was planning to make a trip to South America, and I was scheduled to preach at his church the same night of the baseball game. Almost weeping, I called the company representative back and turned down the tickets.

I don't know if I will ever have another chance to sit in the Super Box or not, but because I am a Christian, some day I shall sit in a place much more wonderful than the Super Box at Yahoo Dome. In Revelation 3:21 the Lord Jesus promised, "To him that overcometh will I grant to sit with me in my throne."

In fact, the Bible teaches that everyone who has been saved by personal faith in Jesus Christ is already seated in heavenly places. God "hath raised us up together, and made us sit together in heavenly places in Christ Jesus" (Ephesians 2:6).

Of course, our physical bodies are still on this earth, but spiritually we are already seated in heavenly places with the Lord Jesus. We may never have the chance to sit in the Super Box at Yahoo Dome, but we are already seated in God's "Super, Super, Super Box."

Ken Board

THE WRONG END OF THE MATCH

It was about six o'clock in the morning. It was cold and still dark. I crawled out of bed, grabbed the matchbox, and headed for the living room to light the kerosene heater. I took a match out of the box and struck it, but the match wouldn't light. No matter how many times I struck the match, it wouldn't light. Each time the match would not light, I became more and more irritated. Finally, I turned on the living room light and looked at the match. No wonder it wouldn't light! I was trying to strike the wrong end of the match.

The person who is attempting to make himself into a righteous person by his own good works is making a similar mistake. It seems that a lot of people suppose that they can become righteous before God by actions such as being kind to others, being charitable, helping their neighbors, and living an honest life. However, in Isaiah 64:6 the Bible declares that in the sight of God, "all of our righteousnesses are as filthy rags." The Bible makes it clear that the only way to become righteous before God is to believe in Christ the Savior that God has sent and to receive Him as our personal Savior.

Of course, good works are important but we must not reverse the order. We do good works not in order to be saved but because we are saved. The good works are the result and the proof of our faith in Christ. The person who reverses the order of faith and works is similar to a person trying to strike the wrong end of the match.

"For by grace are ye saved through faith; and that not of yourselves: it is the gift of God. Not of works, lest any man should boast. For we are his workmanship, created in Christ Jesus unto good works, which God hath before ordained that we should walk in them" (Ephesians 2:8–10).

"NO, WALLY, NO!"

My daughter has a cat named Wally. I don't know why, but Wally is fascinated by bags containing loaves of bread. If we don't put the bread away before we go to bed, when we awake the next morning, the bag will be torn and the bread will be scattered all over the place.

When that happens, I grab Wally, set him down in front of the torn bag, and say, "No, Wally, no!" And then, because we received Wally from a Japanese friend, I say the same thing to him in Japanese. However, neither the English nor the Japanese is having any effect, for if Wally has the opportunity, he will play with the bags of bread.

On one hand, it would be good for Christians to be like Wally and be as fascinated with the Word of God as Wally is fascinated with the bags of bread. The Lord Jesus said, "Man shall not live by bread alone, but by every word that proceedeth out of the mouth of God" (Matthew 4:4).

On the other hand, it would not be good for Christians to be like Wally, for even if he is able to get the bread out of the bag, he doesn't eat it. He just leaves the bread scattered around with claw marks in it.

There may be Christians who treat God's Word, the Bread of Life, in the same manner. They have a Bible and could partake of the Bread of Life daily, but from Sunday to Sunday the Bible just sits on a bookshelf.

Of course, after Wally opens the bag of bread and plays with it, the bread becomes a loss to my family. Likewise, the Christian who opens his Bible only when he attends church is suffering a great loss.

Ken Board

THE PUMP WAS IN THE WRONG CAN

It was quite cold that Sunday morning, so as soon as I arrived at church, I lit both of the kerosene heaters. I checked the tanks and both of them were almost empty, so I brought in one of the cans of kerosene and put the hose into the heater tank and turned on the pump. There wasn't much kerosene left in that can, so it ran out right away.

I brought in the other kerosene can, turned the pump on, and waited for the tank to fill. Normally, it fills quickly, but a couple of minutes passed and it still wasn't full. I pulled the pump out of the tank, checked to make certain it was working properly, put it back into the tank and turned it on, but a couple of minutes passed and the tank still wasn't full. Wondering what in the world the problem might be, I turned around and saw that I still had one end of the pump in the empty can. I had forgotten to take it out of the empty can and put it in the full one.

As I considered my embarrassing mistake, I was reminded of some of the experiences of my Christian life, especially the times when I tried to help other people with their problems but didn't have the power to do so. For example, I tried to comfort those who were sorrowing and found that I had no power to comfort them, or I tried to win someone to Christ only to realize that I didn't have the power to lead him to the salvation that is in Christ.

Just as the tank of a kerosene stove becomes empty, from time to time the tank of our spiritual power becomes empty. We want to work for the Lord, but there just doesn't seem to be sufficient power in us to do the work that the Lord has led us to do. When our tank of spiritual power has become empty it is very important that we fellowship with the Lord through prayer. In Acts 4:31 we read, "And when they had prayed, the place was shaken where they were assembled together; and they were all filled with the Holy Ghost." Verse 33 tells us the result. "And with great power gave the apostles witness of the resurrection of the Lord Jesus."

Before we leave our room each morning, let's spend time in prayer and refill our tanks of spiritual strength in order to witness with great power to the people that we shall meet that day.

The Amusings of a Missionary

THE CAT'S RESENTMENT

My daughter found a puppy at the park. The puppy lived with us for three weeks before we could find someone to take him. Of course, during those three weeks we had to take the dog for a walk several times a day. When we took the dog outside, we didn't put him on a leash, so he was free to run around the yard. However, whenever we took the cat outside, we always put a leash on him so he wouldn't run away.

There were two reasons why we let the dog run free but put a leash on the cat. First of all, the dog wouldn't leave the yard, but if we let the cat out without a leash, the cat would go in the yards of other homes or out into the street. Also, when we called the dog, the dog would come back right away, but no matter how many times we called Wally, he wouldn't return until he was ready to come back.

The cat just couldn't seem to understand why he had to be on a leash but the dog could run free. The cat began to resent both me and the dog. Wally looked at the dog with a piercing stare and accused me with his eyes and his pitiful cries. It was as if he were saying, "That dog doesn't even belong to you and you let it run freely. I am the pet of this house, but you won't let me run around freely."

Perhaps there are times when our attitude becomes an attitude that resents the Lord like Wally resented the dog and me. "Lord, you answered the prayer of that Christian. Why won't you answer my prayer? Lord, you blessed that Christian abundantly. Why won't you give me the same blessings?"

In John 8:31-32 the Lord Jesus said, "If ye continue in my word, then are ye my disciples indeed; And ye shall know the truth, and the truth shall make you free." The extent of our freedom and our blessings will be determined by our obedience to the voice of the Lord or by our disobedience that ignores the voice of the Lord.

Ken Board

PUSH THE BUTTON

I headed for the hospital to visit my wife, who was expecting our fourth child soon. I entered the elevator and pushed the Close button. Deep in thought, I stood there for two or three minutes before I realized that the elevator had not moved. I had pushed the button to close the door but had forgotten to push the button for the fourth floor. I was glad there was no one else in the elevator. Please allow me to use this embarrassing incident to relay an important message to those who have yet to receive the Lord Jesus Christ as their personal Savior.

Perhaps you attend church regularly and have heard the gospel many times. Perhaps you understand that you are a sinner in the eyes of God. Perhaps you understand that Christ died for your sins on the cross. Perhaps you even understand that if you will admit to God that you are a sinner and receive Christ as your Savior, all of your sins will be forgiven and you will become a child of God.

However, even if you have a mental knowledge of these important truths and understand what you need to do to be saved, until you take the next step, you are similar to a person who is on an elevator that is not moving. The next step is to push the button of faith. According to the Bible, the Lord Jesus wants to save you from the penalty of your sins and lead you into a life of joy and purpose. In John 4:24 Christ said, "He that heareth my word, *and believeth* on him that sent me, hath everlasting life, and shall not come into condemnation; but is passed from death unto life" (emphasis added). Today, believe in the Lord Jesus and accept Him as your personal Savior. The instant you do so, you will find yourself on God's elevator that will take you all the way to heaven.

SAFE OR OUT?

It was the bottom of the tenth inning, the score was tied, the bases were loaded, and there was only one out. If the runner on third scored, the team from the island of Kyushu where I live would win the Japan High School Baseball Championship. The batter lifted a fly ball to right field.

Exactly at this moment I was listening to the game on my car radio. The announcer stated that the fly ball was deep enough to be a sacrifice fly that would score the runner on third base. I began shouting, "We won! We won! The team from Kyushu won!" However, the throw from the right fielder came straight like an arrow into the catcher's mitt and the runner was tagged out. It was one of the most dramatic plays in the history of high school baseball in Japan.

The next morning's newspaper carried a picture that had captured the drama of that play at the plate. Sitting on the ground, the runner was holding both hands in the air. Grasping the ball tightly, the catcher was holding his mitt in the air. Both of them were staring intently at the umpire. In that instant both runners and forty-eight thousand spectators lost interest in everything else and held their breath as they waited for the umpire's decision.

The Bible states that each Christian "must appear before the judgment seat of Christ; that every one may receive the things done in his body, according to that he hath done, whether it be good or bad" (2 Corinthians 5:10). The soul of the person who has received Christ as his personal Savior is eternally safe, but his deeds after he becomes a Christian will determine whether or not he receives a reward from the Lord.

On that day when we appear before the judgment seat of Christ, just like the ballplayers and the spectators who during those few seconds lost interest in everything else and centered all of their concern on the judgment of the umpire, we'll stare into the face of the righteous Judge and wait for His decision. Therefore, let's be diligent in righteous deeds and our work for the Lord in order that our rewards will be "safe" and not "out."

Ken Board

THE UNSTABLE TRASH CAN

The church at which I was scheduled to preach the next day provided lodging for me in a hotel. Except for the trash can, everything about the room was fine. I had some trash in my pocket and in my carry-on luggage, so I moved the trash can from under the desk and placed it near my bed and put the trash inside it.

Later I bumped into the trash can. It fell over and dumped out all the trash on to the floor. Griping at myself for my clumsiness, I stood the trash can up, picked up the trash, and put it into the trash can again. If this had happened just one time, there would have been no problem, but if I even just barely touched the trash can, it would fall over again.

After I had picked up the trash for the third time, I turned the trash can over and looked at the bottom. No wonder it kept falling over. The bottom of the trash can was round, so it would fall over at a touch. I wondered why a company would make a trash can that would fall over so easily.

Later I noticed something under the desk in the spot where the trash can had been. I went closer and looked and saw that it was the base for the trash can. When I moved the trash can near to my bed, I had removed it from its base. When I returned the trash can to its base, it did not fall over again.

Just as a round-bottom trash can will fall over easily when it is separated from its base, a Christian life that is separated from its foundation, the Word of God, will collapse quite easily. A Christian who doesn't open his Bible from one Sunday to the next Sunday is a like a round trash can with no base. As soon as he bumps into some sort of trial, he will collapse. That's why it is vital for a Christian to live a life that is firmly connected to the Word of God. According to Colossians 1:22–23, the Christian who will be "holy and unblameable and unreproveable" in the sight of the Lord is the Christian who will "continue in the faith grounded and settled, and be not moved away from the hope of the gospel."

IT WAS WORTH THE WAIT

Every second and fourth Saturday I teach an English class at a nearby church. There is a time of fellowship after the class, but after all the students leave, I remain and have lunch with the pastor and his family and then play with their two small daughters for a while. Usually, there are some preparations that I must make for the next day's service, so I go home about two o'clock.

One Saturday about two o'clock the pastor's wife said, "Today one of the young ladies of the church is going to made some pudding and bring it to church. It's very delicious. Won't you stay and have some with us?" This young lady's desserts are famous, and I had eaten some before and knew how delicious they were, so even though I had a three o'clock appointment, I decided to wait on the pudding.

At fifteen minutes past two the pudding had not come yet. The pastor's wife said, "She will come soon. Please wait." So I decided to wait a little longer.

At two-thirty the pudding still had not arrived, but the pastor's wife insisted, "It's very delicious pudding," and convinced me to wait a little longer. Finally, about two forty-five, the young lady arrived with the pudding. When I ate it, it was as delicious as the pastor's wife had said it would be and even more so.

Just as I was looking forward to the pudding, Christians are looking forward to the blessings that God is preparing for us in heaven. However, in the time of trial, there is a tendency for us to lose sight of heaven, but just as the pastor's wife encouraged me to remain at church with the words, "The pudding will come soon," the Word of God encourages us with these words, "Be ye also patient; stablish your hearts: for the coming of the Lord draweth nigh" (James 5:8).

When that day comes and we are finally able to enter heaven, just as the young lady's pudding was even more delicious than I had imagined, we will discover that heaven is a much more wonderful place that we had even imagined. "But as it is written, Eye hath not seen, nor ear heard, neither have entered into the heart of man, the things which God hath prepared for them that love him" (1 Corinthians 2:9).

Ken Board

THE PASTOR'S LOSS

The pastor and I loaded several Sunday school children into my van and his car and headed out to a church member's farm to dig potatoes. As we approached the tollbooth for the city expressway, I decided to pay the pastor's toll too. The toll for one vehicle was 360 yen, so I handed the attendant 720 yen and said, "I want to pay the toll for the car behind me too." As I pulled away from the toll booth, I glanced in the rearview mirror, but the car behind me wasn't the pastor's car. Instead of following me, he had decided to go through the other tollbooth. Because he didn't follow me, he lost 360 yen.

There are Christians, too, who suffer loss because they do not follow the Lord. According to the Bible, God rewards our obedience. Moses said to the children of Israel, "Behold, I set before you this day a blessing and a curse; a blessing if ye obey the commandments of the Lord" (Deuteronomy 11:26–27). This principle—namely that rewards follow obedience—is repeated constantly in the Word of God. For example, in Isaiah 1:19, "If ye be willing and obedient, ye shall eat the good of the land," and, in Jeremiah 38:20, "Obey, I beseech thee, the voice of the Lord, which I speak unto thee: so it shall be well unto thee, and thy soul shall live."

I suppose the pastor did not follow through the same tollbooth because he did not know that I intended to pay his toll too. However, because we know that obedience produces blessings, when we do not follow the leadership of the Lord, we may suffer a loss much greater than just 360 yen.

YOU ARE THE PEPPER OF THE EARTH

While my wife has been away in the States, I have been eating a lot more fruit. Especially during these hot summer days I have been eating a lot of watermelon. When I eat watermelon, I always put it in the refrigerator to cool for a while, and then before I eat it, I sprinkle salt on it, for the salt makes it taste much sweeter.

One night when I was watching television, I decided I wanted some watermelon, so I brought a piece of watermelon and some salt to the living room, sprinkled some salt on the watermelon, and lifted it to my mouth. However, just before I put the watermelon into my mouth, I looked at it and was surprised. There were a lot of small black specks on the watermelon. I thought, "What in the world is this?" When I examined the watermelon, right away I realized what had happened. In my haste to get back to my TV program, I had grabbed the wrong shaker and sprinkled pepper on my watermelon. Before I could eat it, I had to try to scrape off all the pepper.

The word *salt* appears in the Bible over fifty times, but the word *pepper* does not appear even once. Of course, one of the more famous passages that contain the word *salt* is Matthew 5:13: "Ye are the salt of the earth." Two other passages that are not quite as famous also compare us to salt. In Mark 9:50 the Bible says, "Salt is good: but if the salt have lost his saltness. Wherewith will ye season it? Have salt in yourselves, and have peace one with another." We who confess the Lord Jesus as our Savior should live a life that looks as delicious to others as a piece of watermelon with salt sprinkled on it in order to have them think, "That way of life looks good. I think I'll try it too."

Also, according to Colossians 4:6, Christians should speak words that have been seasoned with salt. "Let your speech be always with grace, seasoned with salt." No Christian would want the Lord to say of his life, "You are the pepper of the earth," so let's manifest before the people around us a way of living that will attract them to the Lord.

Ken Board

IS IT RED OR IS IT GREEN?

I was on my way home from the Fukuoka airport when I came upon a traffic signal that was hard to understand. The top part of the signal was red. However, underneath the red light there were two green lights, a green arrow pointing straight and another green arrow pointing to the left.

The closer I got to that signal, the more confused I became. "Is it red? Is it green? Can I go ahead? Am I supposed to stop?" I slowed down and got ready to stop, but the car beside me went through the light without stopping, so I did too.

Later I figured out the meaning of that signal. The red light was for cars that wanted to turn right. (We drive on the left side in Japan.) The green lights were for drivers who wanted to go straight or turn to the left. I understand now, but that signal is difficult to understand when a driver sees it for the first time.

Thank the Lord the signal for world evangelization is not a signal that is hard to understand. In Matthew 28:19 the Lord Jesus said, "Go ye therefore, and teach all nations," and in Mark 16:15 He commanded, "Go ye into all the world and preach the gospel to every creature."

There is no need for the church to be confused about world missions. There is also no need to hesitate. Christ declared, "It's not red. It's green. Go! Go! Go!"

In the teachings of the Bible concerning world evangelization, there are no red lights or yellow lights, so let's take our foot off the brake and through ardent prayer and generous offerings go forward for the furtherance of the gospel (Philippians 3:13–14).

60 YEN SHORT

I needed to stop at the gas station and get some gasoline and kerosene, but I had only 4,000 yen (about $40) with me. The gas would cost 140 yen a liter and a can of kerosene (18 liters) would cost 1,170 yen, so I calculated that twenty liters of gasoline (about five gallons) and a can of kerosene would cost 3,970 yen. I pulled into the gas station and asked the attendant to give me twenty liters of gasoline and one can of kerosene. After he had put the gas into the tank and loaded the can of kerosene into the car, he handed me a bill for 4,060 yen.

I was confident that my calculation was correct, so I asked him, "Why is it 4,060 yen? It should be 3,970 yen."

He replied, "The price of kerosene went up two days ago. It's now 1,260 yen a can."

Rather embarrassed, I said to him, "I have only 4,000 yen, but I'll go home and get 60 yen and bring it right back to you."

He agreed, so I drove home, got 60 yen from my wife, and hurried back to the station. If I had not been a ten-year customer of that stand, I don't know what the attendant would have done.

Hebrews 9:27 tells us that two things are appointed unto men—death and judgment. The Bible makes it clear that after death all men must stand before God and be judged. The important thing is to make preparation for the judgment before we die. We must not think that what worked with the gas station attendant will work with God. We may plead, "God, I'm sorry. I'm not quite ready to be judged. Please permit me to return to the earth for a while," but it will be too late. That's why the Bible warns us to "prepare to meet thy God" (Amos 4:12).

Ken Board

THE FUTON COVER

During the Bible conference we borrowed futons from our church members to provide lodging at the church for several people. When I went to return the futons, one lady said to me, "This is not my futon. The cover is the same, but the futon is different." To me the futons all looked the same, but the lady knew her own futons, so right away she knew that the futon that I had brought to her home was not her futon.

It was an incident that reminded me of the condition of present-day Christianity. There are people who insist, "I too am a Christian," and they use words like *church* and *faith* and *Jesus*, but they are not true Christians. Like the lady's futon, the cover is the same, but the content is different. The Bible warns us about these people in 1 John 4:1: "Beloved, believe not every spirit, but try the spirits whether they are of God: because many false prophets have gone out into the world."

Even though the "cover" of their faith may be the same, let's check the content by asking three questions.

First, "What do you believe about the Bible?" (The Bible is the inspired Word of God without error or contradiction—2 Timothy 3:16–17).

Second, "What do you believe about Jesus Christ?" (Jesus Christ is the sinless, virgin-born Son of God who died on the cross for our sins and arose bodily from the dead on the third day—1 Corinthians 15:1–4).

Third, "What do you believe about the way of salvation?" (A person is saved by God's grace through personal faith in Jesus Christ—Ephesians 2:8; Galatians 3:26).

Usually, a person's answers to these three questions will reveal if he is a true believer or not, so let's "try the spirits" and not be deceived by just the cover.

100 PERCENT, 50 PERCENT, 10 PERCENT

At my house we don't need to look at a calendar to know what week of the month it is. We can easily know that just by looking at the orange juice container. If it is the first or second week of the month just after our monthly support has arrived, we drink 100 percent orange juice.

As the money begins to decrease, the orange juice changes. By the third week, my wife is buying 50 percent orange juice, and in the last week of the month when the money is almost all gone, we drink 10 percent orange juice.

According to Mark 4:16–17, our Christian life, too, can be divided into three distinct periods. "And these are they likewise which are sown on stony ground; who, when they have heard the word, immediately receive it with gladness. And have no root in themselves, and so endure but for a time: afterward, when affliction or persecution ariseth for the word's sake, immediately they are offended."

The first period of our Christian life is filled with joy. We enjoy going to church. We enjoy reading the Bible. We enjoy being a witness of the gospel to others.

In the second period of our Christian life, we are still attending church, but the joy is only about half what it once was.

In the third period of our Christian life, we attend church only now and then, and our joy is now down to only 10 percent of the joy we experienced in the first period.

Why? Why has the joy of our life of faith decreased from 100 percent to 10 percent? Exactly as it is written in Mark 4:17, the problem is a "root" problem. According to Colossians 2:7, a Christian should be a person who is "rooted and built up in Christ." If we have daily fellowship with Christ through prayer and the Bible, we can remain in the first period of the Christian life and continue to enjoy 100 percent spiritual fruit.

I wrote this message on the sixth day of the month. This morning we had 100 percent orange juice for breakfast. I wonder what week of the month it is in your spiritual life right now.

Ken Board

WHY DOESN'T SOMEBODY ANSWER THE PHONE?

When I called the Missions Office in America, the phone rang several times, but no one answered. It seemed strange to me, because usually when I call, the receptionist answers right away. I thought, "Maybe I dialed the wrong number," so I called again. The phone rang five, six, seven times, but no one answered.

I had something important to tell the Missions Office, so I became more and more frustrated when no one answered my call. I complained, "Why won't somebody answer the phone? What in the world is the receptionist doing?"

Just then I happened to glance at an American calendar on my desk, and I immediately realized why no one would answer the phone. It was an ordinary day in Japan, but it was a holiday in America. The Missions Office is always closed on holidays.

I was able to make contact with the office the next day, but through my frustration of the previous day, I have become thankful of the fact that there are no holidays in heaven. When I call upon the name of the Lord, I never get an answering machine that says, "We're sorry, but God is off today. Please call back tomorrow."

According to the Bible, when we call upon the name of the Lord, He will answer without fail. In Psalm 86:7 David wrote, "In the day of my trouble I will call upon thee: for thou wilt answer me."

No matter what time of the day or what day of the month it may be, the Lord will answer the calls of those who believe in Him. Because we are confident of this, our hearts can be at ease. "Evening, morning, and at noon, will I pray, and cry aloud: and he shall hear my voice" (Psalm 55:17).

THE UNLIT STOVE

Although Kyushu is in southern Japan, the weather becomes quite chilly in the winter months. On cold days there is a young man in the church who comes early and lights the heaters, but one very chilly day he wasn't able to come early. When I unlocked the door, two of the young ladies rushed to the stove to warm their hands. When I entered the room and saw the two of them holding their hands over the stove, I couldn't help but laugh. The stove wasn't lit.

The image of the two of them trying to warm their hands over an unlit stove is an image of the spiritual condition of many people. They sense a spiritual coldness and search for something to warm their hearts. They try philosophy, knowledge, possessions, pleasure, or social position only to discover that these things are of no more assistance to a cold heart than an unlit stove to cold hands.

The testimony of the two men who were on the road to Emmaus in the twenty-fourth chapter of Luke reveals the source of warmth for the heart. After walking with the Lord Jesus and listening to Him expound the Scriptures, they exclaimed, "Did not our heart burn within us, while he talked with us by the way, and while he opened to us the scriptures?" Fellowship with the living Christ through the Word of God is the only source of warmth for the soul of a man.

The Lord Jesus told us in Matthew 24:12, "Because iniquity shall abound, the love of many shall wax cold." The conditions of modern society manifest the fulfillment of this prophecy, so let's be careful lest we try to warm our hearts over an unlit stove.

Ken Board

THE TRASH IN THE CORNER

After Sunday school and church, we had lunch together, and then it was time to clean the church before we went home. One of the young ladies saw some trash on the floor, so she grabbed the broom and began sweeping. One of the children saw her and said, "Let me do it." She took the broom and began sweeping as hard as she could. However, I noticed that instead of sweeping the trash into one spot where it could be picked up by a dust pan, she was sweeping it toward the corner of the room.

When I asked her, "What are you doing?" she replied, "I'm putting the trash where it won't be seen."

Her words and action reminded me of a tendency that can be seen in my own life and in the lives of many Christians. How often we spruce up our outward appearance by hiding the "trash" in our heart. Through the diligence of our ministry and the skillfulness of our words we make an effort to put on as good a front as possible while sweeping the sins of our life into one corner of our heart.

Let's learn the sobering truth found in 1 Samuel 16:7: "The Lord seeth not as man seeth; for man looketh on the outward appearance, but the Lord looketh on the heart." Hebrews 4:13 teaches us, "Neither is there any creature that is not manifest in his sight: but all things are naked and opened unto the eyes of him with whom we have to do." Also, we must not forget the day is coming when God will "judge the secrets of men" (Romans 2:16). On that day the Lord will bring out into the light the hidden things of darkness and reveal every corner of our heart.

Therefore, we are faced with two choices. Like the child at my church, we can sweep the sins of our life into a corner of our heart and try to hide them. Proverbs 28:13 shows us the folly of this choice: "He that covereth his sins shall not prosper."

Our other choice is the prayer that David prayed in Psalm 19:12: "Cleanse me from secret faults."

1,200 YEN FOR 700 YEN WORTH OF FOOD

The cost of the all-you-can-eat breakfast at the hotel was 1,200 yen (about $12), so the pastor, his daughter, the young church member, and I created mountains of the delicious food on our plates.

When the young man finished his first plate of food, he sighed, "I'm full."

I replied, "Full? You can't be full yet. This meal costs 1,200 yen. You have eaten only 700 yen worth. Hang in there."

He immediately got up and went to fill up his second plate. Actually, I was kidding with him, but when you pay for an all-you-can-eat meal, don't you feel obligated to keep eating until you just can't eat another bite?

Christians need to remember that the delicious spiritual food that God has prepared for us in His Word is "all-you-can-eat"; therefore, when we read the Bible in any of the following three ways, we are similar to the young man who ate only about 700 yen of a 1,200-yen meal.

First: reading the Bible out of a sense of duty. The Christians who spend five minutes a day reading the Bible because they "have to read the Bible" are settling for five minutes of blessings when they could enjoy so much more. Perhaps if we reduced our TV time, we could read the Bible long enough for our heart to overflow with blessings.

Second: reading the Bible too rapidly. Of course, a goal of reading the Bible through in one year is an excellent goal, but if we read it too rapidly merely for the purpose of reaching a goal, we won't be able to receive the full benefit of the blessings God has prepared for us in His Word.

Third: reading just enough to prepare for our ministry at church, for example a sermon or a Sunday school lesson. One of the purposes of our ministry should be to be a blessing to those who sit under our ministry, but before we can share a blessing with others, there is a need first of all to fill our hearts to overflowing with the blessings the Lord has provided in His Word, and then as a natural result, those blessings will flow out to others.

If you have already read the Bible today and eaten your first plate of spiritual food, why not go back for the second plate? After all, it's all-you-can-eat.

"I am the Lord they God: open thy mouth wide, and I will fill it" (Psalm 81:10).

Ken Board

THE NEWSPAPER CLIPPING
THAT SADDENED ME

Before my mother went home to be with the Lord, she wrote me a letter every week without fail. Occasionally, she would include a clipping from my hometown newspaper. For example, recently I received an article about my aunt who had just turned one hundred years old.

The other day I received a clipping that made me sad. It was a picture of a junior high school being torn down. The city planned to build a new $6.5 million school at that location, so they had to tear down the old school that was built in 1923.

Of course, I am happy for the students who will be able to attend the new school, but that old school was a place of many good memories for me, so I was somewhat saddened by the news. Now neither my home nor my school remains in the town where I was raised (Roanoke, Virginia).

However, because I have believed in the Lord Jesus and have received Him as my personal Savior, I have a home that no one will ever tear down. That home is the home that Christ is preparing for all believers in heaven. In John 14:2 the precious words of Christ are written: "In my Father's house are many mansions. I go to prepare a place for you."

The Bible also teaches us that our eternal home will be in a city whose builder and maker is God Himself (Hebrews 11:10). It will be a home where "neither moth nor rust doth corrupt, and where thieves do not break through nor steal" (Matthew 6:20). It will be an incorruptible, undefiled home that will never fade away (1 Peter 1:4).

Therefore, even though we have to live in a world where our homes and our schools will eventually crumble and fall, let us rejoice and be thankful for our eternal home in the city of God.

SIX TIMES TO THE BANK

Because we changed the name of our church, I had to go to the bank to change the name of our account. The first time I went to the bank, I went just to receive the application necessary to change the account name. After I had one of the church members fill out the application, I went to the bank a second time, but there was a mistake on the application.

I received a new application, had one of the church members fill it out, and went to the bank for the third time. I was told that we needed one more document, so I received the document, had one of the church members fill it out, and went to the bank for the fourth time. We had made a mistake on the document, so I received a new document, had one of the church members fill it out, and went to the bank for a fifth time. However, I forgot to take our old ATM card with me, so I was told to come back and bring the card with me. Finally, on the sixth try, I was able to have our account name changed.

Just imagine what it would be like if going to heaven were this complicated.

The first time: "God, please let me into heaven." "Have you read all of the Bible?" "No." "Sorry, you can't come in."

The second time: "Do you pray at least one hour every day?" "No." "Sorry, you can't come in."

The third time: "Have you attended church for at least six months without missing even one time?" "No." "Sorry, you can't come in."

The fourth time: "Have you been baptized?" "No." "Sorry, you can't come in."

The fifth time: "Do you tithe?" "No." "Sorry, you can't come in."

The sixth time: "God, I have read all of the Bible, I pray at least one hour every day, I attend church every Sunday, I have been baptized, and I tithe."

"Okay, come on in."

Aren't you thankful that going to heaven is not that complicated? The publican in Luke 18:13 cried out," God be merciful to me a sinner," and in verse 14 it says that he was justified.

Anyone who will repent of his sins and believe in the Lord Jesus can enter heaven. Hallelujah!

Ken Board

I TURNED THE TV OFF
IN THE SEVENTH INNING

With great excitement I turned on the TV to the high school baseball championship game. A team from Kyushu, the area where I live, had reached the final game. However, in the seventh inning the team from Hiroshima took a 4-0 lead, so I sadly turned off the TV. I just couldn't bear to see the team from Kyushu lose.

Later I turned the TV back on again just in time for the championship trophy presentation. I was amazed to see the captain of the team from Kyushu step forward to receive the trophy. I thought, "This can't be! The team from Hiroshima won, didn't it? Don't tell me that the team from Kyushu won!" As I sat there and watched the trophy presentation, I couldn't believe my own eyes.

Later, there was a replay of the highlights, and I found out that the team from Kyushu had scored five runs in the eighth inning for a come-from-behind victory. Furthermore, I learned that the winning runs had scored on a grand-slam home run.

When I realized that the team from Kyushu had won, my emotions were mixed. Of course I was ecstatic. The team from Kyushu had won! However, the level of regret in my heart was about the same as the level of joy. When the team from Kyushu was losing 4-0 in the seventh inning, I didn't have enough faith to believe that they could win the game, so I turned the TV off and missed the opportunity to see with my own eyes the dramatic game-winning grand-slam home run. Half of my heart was happy and the other half was sad.

There are times in our spiritual lives when, because of unbelief, we miss out on a victory or blessing. For example, we pray to the Lord in faith and eagerly await His answer, but when the Lord doesn't reply soon, we quit praying and end up missing out on a great blessing, or perhaps we are placed in some sort of unfavorable circumstance and give up on the Lord's power to deliver us and end up missing out on the opportunity to experience a dramatic victory.

So when our spiritual life is like a team that is losing 4-0 in the seventh inning, let's not make a judgment based on just what we can see at the present time. Instead, let's continue to believe in the power of the Lord to bring us the victory.

"For we walk by faith, not by sight" (2 Corinthians 5:7).

ALL THE LIGHTS WERE RED

After the Wednesday evening service we climbed into our van and headed home. It was about ten o'clock. There are four tollgates on the city expressway, and that time of the night only two of them are open. Usually, the first or second gate from the left is always open, so I headed in that direction. I was startled to see that there were red lights above all four gates. I thought maybe the expressway was closed and I wondered why.

We sat there for about thirty seconds trying to decide what to do when we saw a man hurrying toward one of the gates and then I understood why all the lights were red. We had arrived at the tollgates exactly at the time of the shift change of the tollbooth attendants. As soon as he entered the booth, the light over that gate turned green, and we headed on home.

There are times in the life of a Christian when all the lights are red. When Paul tried to take the gospel to Bithynia, he was stopped by a red light (Acts 16:7). David Livingstone wanted to be a missionary to China, but the light was red.

When all the lights are red, what should the child of God do? He should wait. While praying, "Lord, cause me to know the way wherein I should walk" (Psalm 143:8), he should wait for God's leadership. If we hasten ahead in spite of the red light, we are headed for failure and disappointment. If we wait for a green light from the Lord and then proceed on the path to which He has guided us, we are certain to discover many blessings.

In Psalm 37:23 it is written, "The steps of a good man are ordered by the Lord." There are times when He orders us to go forward, but there are also times when He orders us to stop and wait at a red light.

Ken Board

"PLEASE SHUT THE DOOR AGAIN."

O n the way to the ladies' meeting, we stopped by a lady's house to give her a ride. While we were waiting for her to come out of the house, I got out of the car and opened the back door for her. I was going to close the door for her after she got into the car, but before I could close it, she closed it herself. I returned to the driver's seat and started to pull away, but I noticed the car's interior light was still on, which meant that the door was not closed properly.

I asked the lady to open her door and close it again. She did, but the light still didn't go out. I said, "I'm sorry, but would you shut your door again?"

She opened the door and shut it much harder than before, but the light was still on. I said to her, "Please forgive me, but would you shut your door one more time?" This time she slammed it shut with all of her might, but the light still didn't go out.

Just then I thought to check on my own door and discovered that it was my door that was not closed properly. I apologized to the lady over and over again on the way to church.

Why is it that we always want to make our problems the fault of someone else? This tendency has continued since the time of Adam and Eve (Genesis 3:12–13). The Lord Jesus addressed this tendency with extremely strong words in Matthew 7:3–5: "Why beholdest thou the mote that is in thy brother's eye, but considerest not the beam that is in thine own eye? Or how wilt thou say to thy brother, Let me pull out the mote out of thine eye, and, behold, a beam is in thy brother's eye. Thou hypocrite, first cast out the beam out of thine own eye; and then thou shalt see clearly to cast out the mote out of thy brother's eye."

When we are having conflicts with others, before we make it the fault of the other person, let's make certain that it is not our own door that is open.

MY BATTLE WITH THE MOB OF LADIES

In the eleventh chapter of 2 Corinthians, Paul describes the various perils that he experienced (verses 23–27). The other day I experienced a peril that Paul never experienced even once.

On the day before Valentine's Day, I went to buy my wife and daughter a box of chocolates. Valentine's Day in Japan is quite different from Valentine's Day in America. In America the men and ladies give chocolate to each other, but in Japan only the men receive chocolate on Valentine's Day. (In March there is a day called "White Day" when the men must give something white to all the ladies who gave them chocolate on Valentine's Day.) However, I knew my wife and daughter would be expecting some chocolate from me, so on the thirteenth I went to the department store.

I do not know how to describe adequately the scene near the chocolate counter at the store. It looked like a war was taking place. Ladies were shoving and being shoved. Except for me, there was not another man in sight. Risking my life, I plunged into the mob of ladies, shoved a few of them out of the way, fought my way to the counter, and bought my wife and daughter some chocolate.

The truth is I knew what the situation would be, so I hadn't even wanted to enter the store, but the motivation to plunge into that mob came from my love for my wife and daughter. That love compelled me to go get some chocolate to give to them on Valentine's Day.

When you truly love someone, you can't help but want to give them something that will express your love. True love is giving love. The greatest example of true love is the love of God Himself. "For God so loved the world that he gave his only begotten Son" (John 3:16). God loved each of us so much that He gave us a Savior, His only begotten Son, the Lord Jesus Christ.

If we love God who first loved us, there will be a zealous desire in our heart to give Him something that expresses our love. For example, we should give Him our time and attend church faithfully. We should give Him our money and support the ministry of the church. We should give Him our talent and ability and serve Him at church. So on Valentine's Day, when we give chocolate to others, let's not forget to give God some "chocolate" too.

Ken Board

RAW FISH AND RAW BEEF

*S*ashimi (raw fish) is considered a delicacy in Japan. I have eaten *sashimi* many times. The other night I thought I would have to eat raw beef for the first time.

My wife decided that she wanted to eat *yakiniku* (thin pieces of beef that you fry on an electric hot plate). While the rice was cooking, she cut the meat and vegetables into small slices. When the rice was ready, she called me. I don't care as much for *yakiniku* as she does, for as soon as I pray and say amen, I want to start eating, but when we have *yakiniku*, it takes time for the meat to fry. Another reason I don't care for it very much is I have to fry my own meat.

After I prayed, I placed my meat on the hot plate and waited for it to start frying, but several minutes passed and the meat was still as raw as ever.

My wife said, "That's strange," and checked the hot plate. When she did, she discovered why the meat wouldn't fry. She had turned the hot plate on, but she had forgotten to plug it into the electric outlet. Even if we had sat there and waited all night, the meat would not have fried, because the hot plate was not connected to the electricity.

From time to time there are similar experiences in our spiritual life. We try to carry out the work of the Lord, but we just can't seem to succeed. Could it be because we are not connected to the Lord, who is our source of spiritual power? When we do not regularly fellowship with the Lord through prayer and the Word, we are no different than an electric hot plate that is not connected to the electricity. In John 15:5 the Lord Jesus said, "Without me ye can do nothing." On the other hand, if we maintain a regular time of fellowship with the Lord, we can do all things through Christ who strengthens us (Philippians 4:13).

I wonder what kind of "hot plate" we are at the present time. Are we a hot plate that has spiritual power because we are connected to the Lord through daily prayer and reading of the Word, or are we a hot plate that is ineffective because we are not connected to the power of God?

5:46 A.M.

I turned on the TV at exactly 5:46 a.m. to check the weather report and was surprised to see a scene that resembled a scene from a disaster movie. I thought, "When did this channel start showing movies at this time of the day?" But it wasn't a movie. I was looking at the massive damage caused by an extremely strong earthquake. As I sat there and watched the stunning scenes from the area, several thoughts crossed my mind.

First, I was reminded of the uncertainty of life. In Proverbs 27:1 the Bible says, "Boast not thyself of to morrow; for thou knowesth not what a day may bring forth."

My next thought was the importance of having a place of refuge. When events like this great earthquake—such as death, sickness, accidents, failure, broken hearts, and loss of employment—take place, it is of utmost important that we have a place of refuge for our troubled heart. For the person who believes in the Lord Jesus Christ, there are two facts that provide security in the time of trouble.

One is the absolute presence of God. "God is our refuge and strength, a very present help in trouble. Therefore, will not we fear, though the earth be removed, and though the mountains be carried into the midst of the sea; Though the waters thereof roar and be troubled, though the mountains shake with the swelling thereof" (Psalm 46:1–3). "Yea, though I walk through the valley of the shadow of death, I will fear no evil: for thou art with me" (Psalm 23:4).

The other one is the Word of God. "Heaven and earth shall pass away, but my words shall not pass away" (Matthew 24:35).

It could be that the clock of our life is nearing 5:46 a.m. If so, is our heart ready for what might take place then? Let's hasten to receive the Lord Jesus as our Savior and make Him the refuge of our heart and experience a faith that can withstand the earthquakes of life.

Ken Board

"DADDY, DO YOU LOVE ME?"

My daughter had already finished her supper and gone to her room to play when she suddenly reappeared in the kitchen and asked, "Daddy, do you love me?"

I had just put a spoonful of food into my mouth when she asked her question, so when I didn't answer her right away she asked again, "Daddy, do you love me?"

I hurriedly swallowed my food and replied, "Yes, I love you."

Then she sprang the brilliant trap. "Well, if you really love me, will you take me to the park?"

"Daddy, if you really love me, will you take me to the park?" How closely this resembles some of our prayers to the Lord. "Lord, if you really love me, will you do this for me?" For example, "Lord, if you really love me, will you heal my sickness?" Or, "Lord, if you really love me, will you bless me financially?" Of course, it's okay to ask the Lord to heal our sickness or bless us financially, but we must never doubt the love of God, for the Bible repeatedly declares God's love to us.

For example, "In this was manifested the love of God toward us, because that God sent his only begotten Son into the world, that we might live through him. Herein is love, not that we loved God, but that he loved us, and sent his Son to be the propitiation for our sins" (1 John 4:9–10). In order to save us from our sins, God sent the Lord Jesus to die on the cross for us. Therefore, even if God did nothing else for us, such as heal our sickness or bless us financially, we ought to believe in His love and be thankful.

SWEETIE PIE AND ARIEL

One of my granddaughters named her cat Sweetie Pie, and the other one named her cat Ariel. Both of the cats are similar in appearance, somewhat chubby, but their personalities are completely different. Ariel is quick to meow when he (yes, it's a male cat named Ariel) wants something. For example, when Ariel wants to enter a room where the door is closed, he will sit by the door and yell until someone opens the door for him.

On the other hand, Sweetie Pie rarely meows. If she wants to enter a room where the door is closed, she will sit quietly by the door until someone notices her and opens the door for her. Recently, when I was visiting my granddaughters, they noticed that Sweetie Pie was missing. Two days later my daughter found her locked in the upstairs bathroom. Because she didn't cry for help, no one found her, even though we looked here and there.

The prayer life of a Christian will resemble one of these two cats. We may be like Sweetie Pie and rarely ask the Lord for anything. James 4:2 speaks of the Sweetie Pie kind of Christians: "Ye have not because ye ask not."

In our prayer life let's be an "Ariel" Christian. "Ask, and it shall be given you; seek, and ye shall find: knock, and it shall be opened unto you" (Matthew 7:7). When we find our souls "locked in" by the adversities of life, by prayer and supplication with thanksgiving, let's make our requests known unto God (Philippians 4:6).

Ken Board

THE NAGOYA MARATHON

My wife and I made the ten-hour drive up to Nagoya to participate in a wedding. I am not familiar with the roads in Nagoya, so I had the bridegroom draw me a map from our hotel to the church. On the day of the wedding, we followed the map and headed for the church.

What we didn't know was that the Nagoya Marathon was scheduled for the same day and many of the roads were closed. I had no choice but to follow the directions of the policeman and turn right off of the only road that I knew. I wasn't too concerned, though, because I thought I could turn back to the left soon and return to the road to the church. However, every time I tried to turn left, the road was blocked for the marathon, and we kept going further and further in the opposite direction of the church.

I told my wife, "We may be wandering around the streets of Nagoya during the wedding." Finally, we decided that the only thing we could do was to return to the road on the map and wait for the marathon to finish. Fortunately, the marathon ended in time for us to make it to the wedding.

When we come to a place in the road of life that is blocked, instead of collapsing into a state of panic, let's wait on the leadership of the Lord. When Paul attempted to enter Bithynia in the sixteenth chapter of Acts, the road was blocked, so he went to Troas and waited on the leadership of the Lord. As he waited, a man of Macedonia appeared to him in a vision and said, "Come over into Macedonia, and help us" (16:9).

When the road of our Christian life seems to be blocked, instead of getting all flustered and taking off on roads of our own choosing, let's stop and wait for the Lord to give us direction. There's no need to waste even a day wandering around in "the streets of Nagoya."

"Commit thy way unto the Lord; trust also in him; and he shall bring it to pass" (Psalm 37:5).

"YOU'RE OFF COURSE. YOU'RE OFF COURSE."

R ecently, I bought a portable GPS and attached it to my car without reading the instructions, so I still don't know how to use it very well. I finally figured out how to get it to show my current location, but I haven't learned how to do anything else yet.

The other day when I was at another missionary's home, he noticed the GPS and asked if he could look at it. He looked at it for a few minutes and then asked, "Would you like for me to set it to your home address for you?" Of course, I knew how to get home without a GPS, but I thought it would be fun to listen to the GPS tell me how to get home, so I asked him to go ahead and set it. After he had finished, he explained, "If you push this button, the GPS will guide you home."

When I left his house, I headed for home listening to the instructions of the GPS. However, somewhere along the way I strayed from the course that the GPS had selected, and the next thing I knew, the GPS began repeating, "You're off course. You're off course." Over and over again the GPS said, "You're off course. You're off course." Finally I yelled, "Shut up!" and turned the thing off.

According to the Bible, there is a system like a GPS inside of every Christian. That "system" is God the Holy Spirit. Romans 8:14 teaches us that the Holy Spirit is our guide. When we stray from the path we ought to walk, the Holy Spirit tells us, "You're off course. You've left the right path." I was able to turn my GPS off and go the way I wanted to go, but the Christian can't turn off the voice of the Holy Spirit, so when we hear His voice, the best thing to do is to return to the right path immediately.

"Teach me thy way, O Lord, and lead me in a plain path" (Psalm 27:11).

Ken Board

"MOMMA, MAY I GO TO MY FRIEND'S HOUSE?"

After a delicious meal on Christmas Day, my wife, my son, and I were watching a video in the living room when my daughter walked into the room and asked, "Momma, may I go to my friend's house?" When we looked in her direction, immediately all three of us burst into laughter.

My daughter already had on her coat. She already had on her muffler. She already had on her gloves. She was already holding her friend's Christmas present in her hand. Full of assurance that her mother would give her permission to go to her friend's house, she had already made preparations to go.

Later, as I remembered the incident and laughed some more, I realized that the image of my daughter with her coat, muffler, and gloves already on and the present already in her hand was the image of true faith. That day my little daughter taught me the meaning of "the prayer of faith." She taught me the meaning of the words of the Lord Jesus written in Mark 11:24. "What things soever ye desire, when ye pray, believe that ye receive them, and ye shall have them."

After seeing the preparation that our daughter had already made, it was impossible for my wife to refuse her request, so my daughter's faith was rewarded. Our faith too will be rewarded when our actions manifest assurance in God's ability and willingness to hear and answer our prayers.

"If ye have faith as a grain of mustard seed, ye shall say unto this mountain, Remove hence to yonder place; and it shall remove; and nothing shall be impossible unto you" (Matthew 17:20).

DID I GO TO SLEEP IN KYUSHU AND WAKE UP IN HOKKAIDO?

I looked outside on Sunday morning and was amazed to see the ground covered with snow. I thought, "Is this really Kyushu? Did I go to sleep in Kyushu and wake up in Hokkaido?" The roads were already frozen with the fallen snow, and it was still snowing. We usually take the Kitakyushu City Expressway to church, but I found out that it was closed, so a trip that usually takes forty-five minutes took two hours. While we were at church, it stopped snowing for a while, so I was hoping they would open the expressway, but then it began to snow heavily again, so the trip home took two hours.

Although the snow hampers travel conditions, I think it is wonderful. I especially like to stand at the window and look outside when the snow is falling. It's a lovely scene, but it is a scene that soon disappears when people begin to walk on the snow and cars start driving on it and it turns into an ugly mess.

I am thankful that the beauty and wonder of the Lord Jesus Christ is not like the snow. According to Hebrews 13:8, the Lord Jesus is "the same yesterday, and to day, and for ever." I have been looking at the beauty of Christ for over fifty years and it hasn't faded even one little bit. In fact, His wonder seems to grow more brilliant every day. The beauty of His love, mercy, and grace to me are unchanging. I urge everyone who has yet to receive Christ as personal Savior to turn your eyes upon His beautiful salvation. "One thing have I desired of the Lord, that will I seek after; that I may dwell in the house of the Lord all the days of my life, to behold the beauty of the Lord" (Psalm 27:4).

Ken Board

ORANGE JUICE IN MY COFFEE

As soon as I get up every morning, I follow the same routine. I put water in the coffee pot, turn on the heat, and put some instant coffee in my cup. When the water begins to boil, I pour it into my cup, add some sweetener, open the refrigerator, take out the milk, and pour a little into the cup.

The other day when I followed this routine, I noticed one thing different than usual. After I poured the milk into my cup, I noticed that what I was holding in my hand was not the milk jug but rather the container of orange juice. Yes, I had put orange juice in my coffee. Did you think I drank that coffee with the orange juice in it? Nope. I threw out that coffee and started the routine all over again, except this time I made certain it was milk that I was pouring into the coffee.

It is the normal custom of most people to throw away that which has been ruined or scarred, but the Lord is different. The Lord will give people whose lives have been ruined or scarred another opportunity to be used for His service. When we open the Bible and look at the book of Jonah, we see that Jonah rebelled against the leading of God and tried to go in the opposite direction. As a result of his disobedience, he ended up being swallowed by a great fish that had been prepared by the Lord.

However, the Lord did not cast Jonah away, for when Jonah lifted up his prayer from out of the belly of the great fish, it is written that, "And the word of the Lord came unto Jonah the second time" (Jonah 3:1).

Let us be thankful for this wonderful truth. Even though we may stumble and fail, the Lord will give us another opportunity to serve Him. Of course, when we stumble and fail, the Devil will come and say to us, "You're finished," but we must not listen to him. As it is often said, "The God of the Bible is the God of the second chance."

"AAAH"

When I went to Kyoto to speak at a special meeting, the pastor of the church took his daughter, one of the young men of the church, and me to a nearby hotel for breakfast. The tables were loaded with delicious food, and it was all-you-can-eat buffet style, so all four of us loaded up our plates. (I found it interesting that the first one to go back for seconds was the pastor's daughter.) After he had eaten the first plate of food, the young man went, "Aaah."

I asked him, "Did you say 'aaah' because the food was delicious?"

He replied, "No, I said 'aaah' because I am satisfied."

Indeed it was a delicious meal that satisfied the four of us.

A delicious meal can satisfy the body, but there's not one thing in this world that can satisfy the soul of man. The Lord Jesus said to the woman that he met at the well, "Whosoever drinketh of this water shall thirst again." Even if a man could find something to provide a little satisfaction to his soul, he would soon discover that it was only a temporary satisfaction. There is only one thing that can provide everlasting joy and peace. In Matthew 4:4 the Lord Jesus said, "Man shall not live by bread alone, but by every word that proceedeth out of the mouth of God."

Jeremiah spoke these words to the Lord: "Thy words were found, and I did eat them; and thy word was unto me the joy and rejoicing of mine heart" (15:16). Try feeding your soul with the delicious Word of God, and you too will exclaim, "Aaah."

Ken Board

MY DAUGHTER'S TAMAGOTCHI

For several months my daughter kept pleading for me to buy her a Tamagotchi. (A Tamagotchi is a handheld digital pet housed in an egg-shaped computer. Over seventy million have been sold worldwide.) I was willing to buy her one, but they were so popular that they were hard to find. We would hear rumors that a certain store had Tamagotchis for sale, so we would hurry to the store only to be told that they had already sold out of the toy.

One day we heard that a nearby store was going to give out Tamagotchi coupons, so our daughter and one of her friends lined up at six o'clock in the morning with two thousand other children. Only three hundred Tamagotchis were available, and when the coupon numbers were called out, our daughter and her friend didn't have winning coupons. Then another friend ran over and handed them two of the lucky coupons, so a Tamagotchi came to "live" at our home.

One day my daughter walked into my room and handed her Tamagotchi to me and said, "Daddy, I'm going on a walk. Please take care of my Tamagotchi while I'm gone." I immediately became tense, for if you didn't pay attention to the Tamagotchi and play games with it, it would "die." I thought, "If my daughter's Tamagotchi dies while she's on her walk, what will I do?" I sensed a heavy responsibility.

Just then my daughter walked back into the room and asked me to take care of her friend's Tamagotchi too. Two Tamagotchis!

If you can understand the heavy burden of a father who is trying to keep his daughter's Tamagotchi alive, perhaps you can understand to some small degree the heavy burden of a pastor. If I did not fulfill my responsibility to take care of my daughter's Tamagotchi, I would have to answer to her when she came home, but the pastor who bears the awesome responsibility of taking care of the souls of the people of his church will have to answer to God Himself. A church member who is conscious of the heavy burden of the pastor will follow the admonition written in Hebrews 13:17: "Obey them that have the rule over you, and submit yourselves: for they watch for your souls, as they that must give account, that they may do it with joy, and not with grief."

OH NO! GARBAGE DUTY!

In Japan, twice a week we have to carry our garbage to the corner of the road, put it under a net, and place rocks along the edge of the net so the crows can't get into the garbage and scatter it all across the street. Later we all take turns cleaning up. Whoever has the garbage duty must remove the rocks, fold up the net, sweep, and hose down the street. I returned home one night and found a small red bag sitting on my porch. When I looked inside the bag, there was a small piece of wood, and on the wood it was written, "Garbage duty."

My first reaction was, "Oh no!" Usually my wife would take care of this, but she was in America at the time, so I would have to do it myself. On Monday afternoon and on Thursday afternoon, I carried a broom and a small garbage can down to the corner, removed the rocks, folded up the net, swept the street, and hosed it down.

The ladies in my neighborhood are all zealous cleaners. They regularly clean their yards and the ditch in front of their homes. Certainly, cleaning is important, but yards and ditches are not the only things that need to be cleaned. According to the Bible, there is also a need to clean our hearts. In James 4:8 it is written, "Cleanse your hands, ye sinners; and purify your hearts . . ."

"Hands" represent our actions and "hearts" represent our thoughts. If we want to draw near to God, our actions must be righteous actions and our thoughts must be pure thoughts, so just as we regularly clean our surroundings, let's check and see if there is a need to cleanse our hands and our hearts too.

Ken Board

DAVID AND GODZILLA

Whenever we have a Bible quiz in Sunday school, the pastor enjoys making the children laugh by giving amusing answers to the questions. For example, if the question is, "Where did God put Adam and Eve after He created them?" the pastor will answer "Disneyland."

My favorite one was his answer to the question, "What was the name of the giant who fought with David?" When he replied "Godzilla," the children roared with laughter. However, even some of the children who had been coming to Sunday school for a while were fooled by some of his answers.

If our knowledge of the Word of God is not sufficient, even adults who have been Christians for a number of years may be deceived. Therefore, Paul sent this warning to Timothy: "In the latter times, some shall depart from the faith, giving heed to seducing spirits, and doctrines of devils." Peter issued the same warning in his second epistle: "But there were false prophets among the people, even as there shall be false teachers among you, who privily shall bring in damnable heresies" (2:1).

Well, what's the most effective method of protecting ourselves from the deceptions of false teachers? Before he closed his second epistle, Peter taught us that method. "Grow in grace, and in the knowledge of our Lord and Savior Jesus Christ" (3:18). As we increase our knowledge of the Word of God and learn biblical truth, the instant one of the deceptions of false teachers enter ours spiritual ears, it will sound as strange to us as the pastor's answer of "Godzilla." However, the purpose of the heresies of the false teachers is not to amuse us but rather to deceive us, so let's be faithful in church attendance and daily Bible study that will help us to grow in knowledge.

COUNT TO SIX HUNDRED

All of my close acquaintances know that I enjoy practical jokes. One of my favorite days of the year is April Fools' Day, a day on which I have pulled outrageous tricks such as announcing my marriage to Mrs. *Shigatsu Baka*, which means "April Fool" in Japanese, or announcing to everyone that my daughter was expecting triplets. However, sometimes I carry the jokes a little too far. This was one of those times.

A high school boy had been saved and wanted to be baptized. We didn't have a baptistry in our rented building at the time, so we had to drive about thirty minutes to another church that already had a baptistry. He had never seen a baptismal service before, so on the way I explained the service to him.

This time, however, I added one thing. I told him that after I put him under the water, I would count to six hundred. He didn't say anything, but I noticed his lips moving as he looked at his watch. He was trying to calculate how long it would take to count to six hundred. To make matters worse, I then told him, "One of the reasons the churches in Japan are so small is that we lose a lot of people at baptism." Big beads of sweat broke out on his forehead and began to flow down his face.

I intended to tell him that I was just joking, but when we arrived at church, I became engrossed in my fellowship with the church members and forgot to tell him the truth. The young man walked down into the water actually believing that he would have to try to hold his breath until I counted to six hundred. Of course, I put him down into the water and lifted him up right away. From the look on his face, I judged that if the young man had not been a Christian, he would have karate chopped me to death on the spot.

The remarkable thing concerning the young man's baptism is that he was willing to obey the Lord and be baptized even if it meant risking his life. Oh, that all new Christians would be that sincere about baptism! Baptism is not an option of the Christian life. Also, it's not a decision about which we need to pray. Baptism is a command to be obeyed.

"Repent, and be baptized every one of you" (Acts 2:38).

Ken Board

SELF AND FULL

These days, when I go to the gas station, I have to make a choice. Shall I go to a self-service station or to a full-service station? For many years there were only full-service stations in Japan, but lately self-service stations have been increasing. There are still some full-service stations, and there are some stations that have both self-service pumps and full-service pumps.

I went back to America for a month, and when I returned to Japan, I discovered that the full-service station to which I had been going for many years had been changed to a self-service station. I prefer full-service stations, so I began going to a different station. Of course, the price at the full-service station is a little higher, but they wash my windows, throw away my trash, and check my tires, so I gladly pay the higher price.

In our Christian life, too, we have to make a choice between "self" and "full." The "self" Christian life is the life that we maintain by our own power. The believers who choose this life often become spiritually exhausted and lose the joy of their salvation.

There is a "full" Christian life too. This is a life that is maintained by the power of the Lord Jesus. In John 15:11 Christ said, "These things have I spoken unto you, that my joy might remain in you, and that your joy might be full." In Philippians 4:18 Paul wrote, "But I have all, and abound: I am full."

What about us? Can the full joy of Christ be seen in our life, or has the strain of trying to live the Christian life by our own power emptied us of the joy of our salvation?

"PASTOR, I CAN'T FIND MY SHOES."

When I went to speak in the special meeting at the church in Nagoya, there was an amusing incident. (When you enter this church, you take off your shoes and put on a pair of slippers.) After the service, one of the young people came to the pastor and said, "Pastor, I can't find my shoes."

The pastor asked, "What kind of shoes are they?"

The young man picked up a pair of shoes and replied, "My shoes are similar to these shoes."

The pastor and several of the church people began searching for a pair of shoes like the young man's shoes but were unable to find any. Someone suggested that a person wearing the same type of shoes had probably taken the young man's shoes by mistake.

The pastor tried to think of young people who might wear the same type of shoes, but he couldn't recall anyone who wore similar shoes. Finally, the pastor picked up the shoes and asked the young man, "Are you certain these are not your shoes?" As the young man carefully examined the shoes, his face began to turn red, and with a voice filled with embarrassment, he replied, "These are my shoes." Everyone who heard these words could not help but roar with laughter.

Aren't you thankful that the Lord is not like that young man? In John 10:27 the Lord Jesus declared, "My sheep hear my voice, and I know them." Also, in John 6:37 the Lord promised that "him that cometh to me I will in no wise cast out." Even though there may be times when we forget the Lord, the Lord will never forget us. The life of the Christian who is conscious of this great truth will be a life of great peace and deep assurance.

"I am with you always, even unto the end of the world" (Matthew 28:20).

Ken Board

THE PINK NECKTIE

I led the singing in the last service of summer camp. When I introduced the speaker, I said, "I have a great deal of respect for the camp speaker. There are four reasons. First, he is quite intelligent. Second, he's very skillful at personal evangelism. Third, he understands well the correct method of raising children. Fourth, he has the courage to wear a pink necktie."

In both the third service and the last service of summer camp, the speaker wore a pink necktie. I rarely see pastors wearing pink neckties. Usually, in the world of fashion pink is considered a woman's color, not a man's—especially among the men of my generation. That's why I thought it took a lot of nerve for the speaker to wear a pink necktie twice. Actually, his pink necktie matched his other clothing very nicely, so he looked sharp.

In the Christian life, too, it requires a lot of courage to put on the things that are suitable to a person who has trusted Christ as Savior. According to the Bible, the spiritual fashion of the world is "anger, wrath, malice, blasphemy, filthy communication out of the mouth" (Colossians 3:8).

Of course, a Christian should put off all of these things. In Colossians 3:12 the person who has been made anew by God's grace and mercy is told to "put on mercies, kindness, humbleness of mind, meekness, longsuffering." However, it takes courage to put on these things and go out into the world and live a lifestyle that is different from the lifestyle that is in fashion. When a Christian is strengthened by the power of the Lord and puts on these spiritual garments, it is then that his image becomes a charming image that resembles the image of Christ.

WHAT COLOR ARE HER EYES?

Because the father is an American and the mother is Japanese, when my fourth grandchild was born, we were all wondering, "What color will her hair be? What color eyes will she have?" At first, her hair looked black, but the next day you could see some yellow hairs too.

The color of her eyes was a mystery. She kept her eyes shut the day she was born, so on the second day, my son, his wife, his mother-in-law, and I all wanted to see the color of her eyes. I tried to pry open one eye with my finger, but she kept her eyes closed tightly. Finally, we figured out that she wouldn't open her eyes because the light in the room was too bright, so we closed the curtains and turned out the light.

Right away she opened her eyes. We all gathered around her and tried to see the color of her eyes, but the room was so dark we couldn't tell. Finally, my son said, "I think they're dark blue."

If you can imagine the four of us huddled around my granddaughter trying to see the color of her eyes in a dark room, you should be able to understand the words written in Jeremiah 5:21: "O foolish people, and without understanding; which have eyes and see not." Why is it that some people are not able to see the living God whose existence is made so evident by the things which were created? Why is it that some people are not able to see the truth written in the Bible? Like the four of us trying to see the color of my granddaughter's eyes in a dark room, they are walking in spiritual darkness.

Romans 1:21 teaches us the solemn truth that the person who will not give glory and thanks to the Lord will become vain in his imagination, and his foolish heart will be darkened. Even believers in Christ who desire to know the will of God may find themselves in a dark place because of sins in their life. Therefore, Ephesians 5: 8 exhorts us, "For ye were sometimes darkness, but now are ye light in the Lord: walk as children of light." When we find it difficult to know the will of God, let's open the curtains of our soul and let the light of the Word of God teach us His will.

Ken Board

THE DREADED PHONE CALL

Seven months ago I caused a traffic accident. When I went to the police station, the policeman told me, "Because a person was injured, you will receive five points. Just one more point and you will lose your license, so be careful." For the next seven months I drove carefully, but then I caused another accident. The policeman who came to investigate the accident said to me quite sternly, "The cause of this accident was your carelessness. I'll contact you soon and tell you when to come to the police station."

The next week was a terrible time for me. Every time the phone rang, I would gasp and think, "Oh no! It's the police!"

Every time the doorbell rang, I would think, "Oh no! The police have come to take my license away!"

Whenever I returned home after being out for a while, I would rush to the answering machine to see if there had been a call from the police. Five weeks went by. It was a terrible five weeks. I kept thinking, "When will they come? When will they come?"

The church people tried to encourage me. "If they haven't come in five weeks, they probably won't come." I began to relax just a little. However, when I returned home from church one Sunday evening, there was a call from the police on my answering machine.

The next day I went to the police station. The policeman read the accident statement to me and had me sign it. I sat there waiting in fear and thinking, "I wonder how long I'll lose my license. I wonder how much the fine will be." However, the policeman didn't tell me. He just said, "That will be all for today. Be careful." (Later, I had to attend a safety seminar and take both a written test and driving test to have my license reinstated.)

In the Bible it is written that "we must all appear before the judgment seat of Christ; that everyone may receive the things done in his body, according to that he hath done, whether it be good or bad" (2 Corinthians 5:10). To the people whose deeds have been unrighteous, waiting for that judgment is a time of fear. Hebrews 10:27 speaks of a "fearful looking for of judgment." Therefore, in order that we may appear before the judgment seat of Christ not with fear but with joy, let's do that which is holy and good.

MY GOLD TURNED TO BLUE

Yesterday I went to the driver's license office to have my license renewed. On the way home my feelings were divided into two emotions. Of course, I was happy that I would not have to return to the driver's license office for three more years. (It's a process that takes half a day in Japan.) However, I was also somewhat sad. My sadness was caused by the fact that my gold driver's license had turned to a blue license.

The driver's license office in Japan gives a gold-colored driver's license to all drivers who did not have even one violation during the previous three years. Several of the members of the Kitakyushu and Kokura churches have gold licenses, so I was hoping to receive one too. However, every time I went to the license office to have my license renewed, I had committed at least one violation, so for thirty-five years my driver's license was a blue license.

And then, five years ago when I went to renew my license, I did not have even one infraction during the past three years, so I received a five-year gold license. I was so proud I went around showing it to everyone. However, during the next five years, I caused two traffic accidents, so yesterday my beautiful gold license turned back into an ordinary blue one.

The Bible clearly teaches that a Christian can't lose his salvation, but there are several passages that indicate that a Christian can lose his reward. For example, "Look to yourselves, that we lose not those things which we have wrought, but that we receive a full reward" (2 John, verse 8).

There is this passage too: "Every man's work shall be made manifest: for the day shall declare it, because it shall be revealed by fire; and the fire shall try every man's work of what sort it is. If any man's work abide which he hath built thereupon, he shall receive a reward. If any man's work shall be burned, he shall suffer loss: but he himself shall be saved; yet so as by fire" (1 Corinthians 3:13–15).

Because I was a careless driver, I lost my gold license. Let's be careful lest some carelessness in our walk as a Christian results in the loss of our reward from the Lord.

Ken Board

MY ADVENTURE IN
THE WORLD OF SIMULATION

When my driver's license was revoked and I went to the driver's exam office to have it renewed, one of the tests was a simulation test. When I sat in the seat of the simulator, there was a large screen in front of me, and there was a steering wheel, a gas pedal, and a brake. I immediately became extremely tense because until now, every time I had tried to drive one of these simulators at a video arcade I caused an accident and the game had ended in about one minute.

No sooner had the simulation test began when I ran over a man on a motorcycle. The screen flashed "minus eight points."

I tried to be more careful the second time, but a child ran out in front of me and I couldn't stop in time. The screen flashed "minus seven points."

The third time I intended to drive safely, but I hit another motorcycle. "Minus seven points."

The fourth time was a night scene and I hit someone on a bicycle. "Minus ten points."

Finally, I became accustomed to the simulator and was able to drive somewhat safer on the fifth ("minus one point") and sixth ("minus four points") times. The total was minus thirty-seven points. My grade was just one grade above failure. I was quite embarrassed. However, later I took a test in a real car and I did so well that the exam officer commended my driving.

The Christian life is similar to a driving test. The church service on Sunday is the simulation test. Just as we learn safe driving methods through the simulator, through the church service we learn the methods of spiritual growth, but the real test takes place from Monday to Saturday when we go out into a world that doesn't know God and put into practice the truths that we learn on Sunday.

The Bible says, "Do all things without murmurings and disputing: that ye may be blameless, the sons of God, without rebuke, in the midst of a crooked and perverse nation, among whom ye shine as lights in the world: Holding forth the word of life" (Philippians 2:14–16a).

By all means, we should avoid any "minus" actions that would bring shame to our Lord and to our church, so let's hold tightly on to our faith and the Word of God on which it is founded.

HOW WILL I BE ABLE
TO GET HOME?

I parked my car in the parking lot at the drivers' examination office and hurried inside to take a test to have my driver's license renewed. As I listened to the police officer's instruction to the class, suddenly I was startled to hear these words: "By taking this test you will be able to have your driver's license renewed, but you are not allowed to drive today. If a policeman catches you driving today, there will be a heavy fine and your license will be suspended for a long time." I looked out of the window at my car in the parking lot and thought, "What if they check my license when I leave here today? My license will be revoked again. What am I going to do?"

There was a break for lunch, so I hurried to my car and drove to a nearby department store. I left my car in the parking lot there and took a taxi back to the exam office. I sat in the class thinking, "Everything will be fine," but suddenly I was startled again by the words of the instructor. "I know some of you have parked your cars at the department store, but when you leave today, we are going to catch you."

After the test I returned to my car. To be honest, I wanted to go ahead and drive my car home, but the words of the instructor were echoing in my ears. But if I didn't drive home, how would I get home? I decided to take the train home, so I went into the store and asked the assistant manager, "Is it okay if I leave my car in your parking lot tonight?"

He replied, "Yes, it's okay, but it will be expensive. It would be cheaper to hire a substitute driver."

I asked, "A substitute driver? What's that?" He explained it to me and called a substitute driver for me. Two men showed up in a taxi. I rode in the taxi and one of the men followed us in my car all the way to my house. It was expensive, but it was cheaper than a heavy fine and a lengthy suspension of my driver's license.

Fifty-four years ago I found myself in the same situation, only the home to which I wanted to go was not my own home. It was God's home. I wanted to go to heaven, but according to the sermon of the pastor, because I was a sinner, I was not qualified to go to heaven. That pastor introduced me to Jesus Christ, the sinner's substitute. According to the Bible, the Lord Jesus Christ became our substitute and died on the cross for the sins of the whole world. He will take everyone who believes in Him to God's home.

"For Christ also hath once suffered for sins, the just for the unjust, that he might bring us to God" (1 Peter 3:18).

Ken Board

I COULDN'T STOP
BETWEEN THE RED LINES

When I went to renew my driver's license, because of my age, I had to take some tests to check my reaction time. The first three tests were fairly simple. The fourth one was a little more difficult, but I scored well. The fifth one was the problem.

I sat in a car seat (like the ones you can find in a game center) and grasped a steering wheel. A white line appeared on the monitor in front of me. I was told that this white line represented my car. Every few seconds two red lines would appear on the screen. My task was to move my car as quickly as possible and stop it between the two red lines.

I thought, "If I do this slowly, it will be a piece of cake," but the two red lines appeared for only two or three seconds and then changed to a different spot on the screen, so I had to hurry. There was one other problem. If I went too far when I tried to stop my car between the two red lines, the lines would change to yellow, indicating that I had failed. I didn't have trouble getting my car over to the red lines before they moved to another spot, but time and time again I couldn't stop in time and went too far. My score on this test was my lowest score.

As I was taking this last test, I thought, "This test reminds me of sin."

Many people think, "I'm okay. Even if I commit this sin, I can quit any time I want to quit." Actually, they discover that when they try to quit, they have already gone too far and can't stop. Exactly as it is written in 2 Peter 2:14, they "cannot cease from sin."

To avoid going too far on the path of sin and being unable to stop, let us diligently avoid taking the first step onto that path. "Enter not into the path of the wicked, and go not in the way of evil men. Avoid it, pass not by it, turn from it, and pass away" (Proverbs 4:14–15).

THE POINTS ARE GONE!

In January I caused a traffic accident. In August I caused another accident. As a result, my driving license was suspended temporarily. When my license was returned to me, the officer at the license office said to me, "Right now you have nine points. If you cause no accidents for the next year, the points will return to zero." From that day I began to drive carefully. I especially drove slowly through intersections and crosswalks.

From July of this year I began to count the days until the fourth of August. Finally, it was the day for which I had waited a whole year. However, there was one more challenge waiting for me. That evening I had to drive to Fukuoka Airport to meet a missionary. I thought about telling him, "Please take the train or bus," but I headed for the airport full of tension. When the missionary entered my car, I told him, "In just four more hours my points will return to zero."

After I drove him home and then drove back to my home, it was about 10:15. I parked the car in the driveway and stepped out with a great sigh of relief.

Just as my points returned to zero on August 4, 2008, on August 3, 1955, all of my sins returned to zero. On that day I believed in Christ and was saved by God's grace. When I prayed, "God, I believe in the Lord Jesus. Please forgive my sins," my heart which had been black with many sins became as white as snow.

In the case of my driver's license, the points returned to zero because I made an effort to drive carefully. However, there was nothing I could do by my own efforts to make my sins return to zero. But because the Lord Jesus died on the cross for me, my sins were able to return to zero through His precious blood. "In whom we have redemption through his blood, the forgiveness of sins, according to the riches of his grace. (Ephesians 1:7).

Ken Board

SUPER BOWL MONDAY

Today is the day to which all football fans look forward. Today is Super Bowl Sunday. (Because of the time difference, it is Super Bowl Monday in Japan.) The game will be broadcast live in Japan, so I have been looking forward to this day for quite some time.

However, a couple of days ago a missionary friend called me and asked if it would be okay for him to come to my house and watch it with me. Of course, it is more fun to watch the game with someone, so I readily agreed with his suggestion. But then he told me that he had an English class Monday morning, so he couldn't come until the afternoon. I told him that, instead of watching the live broadcast, I would tape the game and watch it with him when he came.

When the time came for the game to start, I wanted to watch it so much that I could hardly stand it. I thought about taking a look at the score on the Internet every now and then, but I didn't give in to that temptation. I tried to get some work done, but I couldn't concentrate. I kept thinking, "I wonder what's happening in the game. I wonder which team is winning."

Although I was concerned about the score of the game, the Christian does not need to be concerned about the things of the future. We don't have to wonder, "What's going to happen? Who will be victorious? Will God win or will the Devil win?" for the Bible clearly tell us the result of this epic battle.

Certainly, as it is written in 2 Timothy 3:1, "in the last days perilous times shall come," but we know what is going to happen after that. The Devil and his host will gather and make war with Christ, but Christ will be victorious (Revelation 19:11–21). To the person who believes in the Word of God, there is no need whatsoever to be concerned about the outcome of the greatest conflict of all.

SAYONARA, WALLY

This message will be quite different than most of my previous messages. In fact, because I am writing this message with a heavy heart full of pain, it will be one of the most difficult messages I have ever written.

Yesterday our daughter's cat, Wally, was hit by a car and killed. Yes, it's true. The Wally who has appeared in many of these messages is dead. Some people may think it strange for me to be this upset over the death of an animal, but Wally was no mere pet to us. He was like a member of the family.

Especially, the relationship of our daughter and Wally was a relationship that far surpassed the usual relationship of owner and pet. I'll sorrow for a while, but I'll eventually get over Wally's death; however, I'll never get over the tears that flowed from my daughter's eyes and the pain of her heart that she expressed with her words.

To be honest, I am writing this message with a heart filled with anger. First of all, I am angry at the Devil who brought sin into this world, for the Bible says in Romans 5:12 that sin entered into the world and "death by sin." Also, I am angry at the cruelty of death. Yesterday, when I rushed into the office of the veterinarian carrying the bloody body of Wally in my arms, he looked at me and spoke some of the most awful words I had ever heard: "It's too late. He's already dead."

Yes, I was angry at the Devil and I was angry at death, but there was also a sense of thanksgiving in my heart, for according to the Bible, even if we are separated by death for a while, there will be a day of reunion (1 Thessalonians 4:13–18). Will we see Wally again? I really don't know. I'll leave that answer to the theologians. However, I am thankful for God's Word that promises us a meeting with our departed loved ones and friends.

The passage that gives me comfort in this time of sorrow is Revelation 21:4: "And God shall wipe away all tears from their eyes; and there shall be no more death, neither sorrow, nor crying, neither shall there be any more pain: for the former things are passed away." Hallelujah!

Ken Board

"I WANT TO KNOW THE REAL JAPAN"

When Brother Daniel arrived in Fukuoka, immediately he said to me, "I want to know the real Japan." True to his words, he did his best to experience life in Japan. For example, whenever we went to a restaurant, he would always order a Japanese dish. Several times I offered to take him to McDonald's, but he replied, "I can eat that kind of food in America. I want to eat food that we don't have in America."

It just so happened that while Brother Daniel was here, I had to make a trip to Nagashima. On the way I told him, "In Nagashima you will experience the real Japan." Saturday evening we had supper at a Japanese pastor's home and for the first time Brother Daniel ate *sashimi* (raw fish). That night we stayed at the church and for the first time Brother Daniel slept on a futon in a *tatami* (straw mat) room.

Brother Daniel told the Japanese pastor too, "I want to know the real Japan," so on Sunday after church he took Daniel to a sushi restaurant. Instead of letting Daniel order what he wanted, the pastor ordered for him and made him eat all kinds of sushi. Brother Daniel ate sea urchin, octopus, *nattoo* (fermented soy beans), and squid. As each new kind of sushi came, he would look at me and ask, "What is this like?"

I answered, "You said you wanted to know the real Japan. Eat it."

A couple of times he made an awful face, but he ate everything that was put in front of him. Because he wanted to know the real Japan, Daniel ate some things that he didn't want to eat.

If Christians would desire to know the Lord Jesus as much as Brother Daniel desired to know the real Japan, without a doubt our Christian life would be filled with more and more blessings. The apostle Paul wrote, "I have suffered the loss of all things, and do count them but dung, that I may win Christ. . . . That I may know him, and the power of his resurrection, and the fellowship of his sufferings" (Philippians 3:8, 10).

The most blessed Christian is the Christian who will even do things that he does not want to do in order to know the Lord Jesus more personally.

THE RED TRAIN

I live about six hundred miles southwest of Tokyo and know very little about the Tokyo area, so when I was invited to speak at a meeting of ladies from several churches in that area, I asked a pastor friend who is from the church where the meeting was to be held for directions from the Tokyo airport to the church.

I quickly discovered that it would not be a simple trip, for I would have to ride the monorail and then change trains twice. The pastor told me that I could arrive quicker if I took the express train at the second station. I asked him, "How will I know which train is the express train?"

He replied, "It's easy. The express train is the red train."

When I stepped off the train at the second station, there was an announcement that the express train would arrive in two or three minutes, so I hurriedly bought a ticket and rushed to the platform. However, the train that pulled into the station was not a red train. It was a yellow train. As I stood there trying to decide if I should board the train or not, I remembered the words of my pastor friend, "The express train is a red train," so I didn't take the yellow train. The next train that entered the station was a much slower train, but it was headed to my destination, so I boarded it.

When I arrived at my destination, one of the young men of the church was waiting for me at the station. When I asked him about "the red train," he laughed and explained, "The train itself is not red. The schedule for the express trains is written in red letters on the timetable at the station." I was looking for a "red train," but the pastor friend was talking about a schedule written in red letters.

On a daily basis there are misunderstandings in communication between people. If our words are not clear, we may be saying one thing and the other person may be hearing an entirely different meaning. Therefore, let us be thankful for the clear teaching of the Lord Jesus that leaves no room for misunderstanding. In John 5:24 Christ said, "Verily, verily, I say unto you, He that heareth my word, and believeth on him that sent me, hath everlasting life, and shall not come into condemnation, but is passed from death unto life." If our faith is based on these words, we can be assured of the fact that our sins are forgiven and our souls are eternally saved.

Ken Board

PAIN AT TWO IN THE MORNING

A t two o'clock in the morning I heard my daughter's voice, "Daddy, Daddy, I want some juice." I searched for my glasses but couldn't remember where I had left them, so half-blind and still half-asleep, I headed through the darkness toward the kitchen. I hit my left shin on a chair and yelled with pain. I turned in the opposite direction and hit my right shin on another chair. Again I yelled, "Ouch!" I could barely walk, but I made it to the kitchen, poured some juice into a cup, and took it to my daughter. As soon as she drank the juice, she went right back to sleep, but I couldn't get back to sleep for quite a while because of the pain in my shins.

Walking blindly in the darkness can be dangerous, so next time I'm going to find my glasses and turn on the light.

The cause of the pain in our heart may be the same. We are walking in darkness. Why? We may be walking in darkness because we have yet to believe in Christ and receive Him as our personal Savior. In John 8:12 the Lord Jesus said, "I am the light of the world: he that followeth me shall not walk in darkness, but shall have the light of life."

Even though we are Christians, we may be walking in darkness because we are not reading the Word of God sufficiently. According to Psalm 119:105, the Word of God is "a lamp unto our feet, and a light unto our path." There is no necessity whatsoever for a Christian to walk in darkness that brings pain and confusion. If we will follow Christ and read the Bible daily, the Word of God will lighten our path and protect us from the dangers that bring suffering and anguish, so when we are stumbling around like a father walking in the darkness without his glasses at two o'clock in the morning, let's open up the Bible and let God shine His light into our lives.

IT WASN'T A RECEIPT

It was the first day of our evangelistic meeting and the church had a big problem. We didn't have enough money for the love-offering for the guest speaker. We needed 20,000 yen (about $200) more. I would have gladly loaned the money to the church, but it was near the end of the month and I didn't have 20,000 yen. I decided to see if the pastor of the church could loan us the money, but it was the end of the month for him too.

As I sat down at my desk wondering what to do, I noticed an envelope on the desk. I opened it and looked inside and found a letter and a receipt for 24,000 yen. At that time the church was sending support to several missionaries, so I just assumed it was a letter and receipt from the office. I handed it to one of the ladies of the church and asked her to read the letter and then take care of the receipt.

About three minutes later I heard her shouting with joy. "Pastor! Pastor! This is a special offering!"

I said, "You mean it's not a receipt?"

She replied, "No, another church has sent us some support." Everyone who knew of the financial predicament of the church immediately gave thanks to the Lord.

That special offering was precious for three reasons.

First, it told us that other churches were praying for us. Second, it proved that God knew our needs and would provide (Matthew 6:32; Philippians 4:19). Third, it meant that even though our church was just a six-month-old church with a handful of members, our church, too, was loved by the Lord. Hallelujah!

Ken Board

THE PHONE NUMBER WAS WRONG

A young lady who was saved at our church is now doing missionary work with her family in South America. At first her parents were violently opposed to her decision to become a Christian and then a missionary. However, one night her mother came to a special evangelistic service at our church and received Christ as her Savior. I couldn't wait to get home and call her daughter, so as soon as I returned home, I grabbed my phone book, but I couldn't find her number, so I called another pastor and got the number from him.

Regretfully, I was so excited over her mother's salvation that I didn't listen carefully and wrote down the wrong number. When I called, there was no answer. Before I went to bed, I called several more times, but no one answered. The next morning I called again, but there was no answer.

After I arrived at church, I learned that another missionary had already informed the missionary of her mother's salvation. To be honest, I was disappointed. I wanted to be the one who told her the wonderful news.

Even now when I remember this incident, I sense a feeling of disappointment. However, it was my own fault. If I had listened carefully and written down the number correctly, I could have been the one to relay the good news.

Through that incident I learned anew the importance of listening carefully to the words of others. And if it's that important to listen carefully to the words of others, how much more important is it to listen carefully to the words of God. When we mix the words of the Lord with our own emotions and opinions in the way that I mixed my excitement with my desire to contact our missionary, we create situations that lead to mistaken beliefs and mistaken actions.

By all means, let us avoid the sad experience of the people of Israel who "hearkened not, nor inclined their ear, but walked in the counsels and in imagination of their evil heart, and went backward, and not forward" (Jeremiah 7:24).

NINE HOURS IN A HOT CLOSET

Let me introduce you to the newest member of our family. She's a kitten named Button. About two weeks before Wally died, our daughter found the kitten in front of our house. She went from house to house in the neighborhood trying to find someone who would take the cat, but when Wally died, we still had the kitten, so our daughter decided that the kitten would be her new pet, and since the kitten liked to play with buttons, our daughter named her Button.

One Sunday Button had a harrowing experience. I preached at one church in the morning, and then my wife and daughter and I jumped into the car and drove ninety minutes to another church in the afternoon. After church we stayed for a while and did some yard work. On the way home we decided to stop and have supper.

Altogether, we were gone from ten thirty in the morning until seven thirty in the evening. When we walked into the house, we heard Button crying for help. We ran around the house searching for her and finally found her in the closet. Evidently, while my wife was getting ready to go to church, Button had climbed into the closet and was trapped there for nine hours on a day when the temperature was over ninety. Button spent nine hours in a hot closet because she was tempted by her own curiosity.

Many of our painful experiences too can be traced to our curiosity that was tempted by something or somebody, and we find ourselves in a place of suffering that we entered by our own volition. Therefore, the Lord Jesus gave us this warning in Matthew 26:41: "Watch and pray, that ye enter not into temptation: the spirit indeed is willing, but the flesh is weak."

If there are associations or habits that tempt us to enter places where we ought not to go, with God's help let's discontinue those habits and associations before we end up in a predicament like the one Button experienced.

Ken Board

"DADDY, LET ME HELP!"

I t was a beautiful Saturday morning, so I decided to wash the car. I got out a bucket, some soap, and a brush, sprayed the car with water, and began washing. When my daughter, who was playing outside at the time, spotted me washing the car, she came running and said, "Daddy, let me help!"

My first thought was, "Oh no! If she helps, it will take twice as long." However, I am hoping for the day when she will take over this job, so I decided this would be a good time to begin to teach her how to wash a car. She took the brush from me, dipped it into the bucket, and began washing as hard as she could. When she finished one side, half of it was clean and half of it was still dirty, so I took the brush from her and washed that side again. We followed this routine for the back, the other side, and the front too, and when we finished, the car was spotless.

In Ephesians 5:25–27 we read, "Christ loved the church and gave himself for it; that he might sanctify and cleanse it with the washing of the word, That he might present it to himself a glorious church, not having spot, or wrinkle, or any such thing; but that it should be holy and without blemish." At the present time, the church is like a car washed by my daughter. It still has many spots and blemishes. It's nowhere near perfection yet. In the church there are hypocrites. In the church there are people whose current lifestyles are not pleasing to the Lord. The church still has many worldly wrinkles in it. However, the day is coming when the Lord will wash His church with the Word, and it will be a glorious church without spot or blemish. Everyone who is involved in full-time ministry at a church embraces this promise and looks forward to the day when his church will be presented to the Lord in holiness and glory.

FUN AT THE MALL

A new mall opened recently near the church. Almost all towns of any size in America have one or more malls, but this mall was the first one built in Kitakyushu City, a city of more than one million people. You'll never guess what they named it. It's called "The Mall."

Shopping is not on my list of favorite things, so malls have little appeal to me. Even when I do go to a mall, I spend all of my time either at a bookstore or an electrical appliance store. However, there is one thing at the mall I like. In fact, it is my favorite way of spending time at a mall. It is watching people.

Therefore, when my wife and daughter asked me to take them to the new mall, as soon as we arrived there and decided on a place and time to meet, I spent about five minutes at a computer store and then found a bench and began watching people. People are fascinating. There are the husbands who very obviously have been dragged reluctantly to the mall by their wives. There are the young couples holding hands. There are people who walk quickly as if they were escaping a fire, and there are others who walk slowly, looking in the window of each store.

There are children who are crying in order to persuade their mother to buy them a new toy, and there are children who leave with a big smile on their face as they tightly clutch the bag holding the latest game.

Their faces, their clothes, and their way of walking all are different, but all of them have one thing in common. All of them have a soul that will live forever. As I sat on the bench and watched them go by, I was thinking, "All of these people, without exception, will go either to hell or to heaven."

This is a fact that Christians should constantly keep in mind: "All of the people around me, all of the people with whom I have regular contact, will believe in Christ and go to heaven, or they will reject Christ and go to hell. It's one or the other."

When Paul considered this fact, he wrote, "I am made all things to all men, that I might by means save some" (1 Corinthians 9:22). Being ever conscious of the eternal soul that dwells in every person we meet, let's be diligent in evangelism.

Ken Board

IT LOOKED DELICIOUS

The week before last I didn't feel well on Tuesday and Wednesday. I had been extremely busy the previous week and then had gone to Oita for the dedication of a new church building, so when I awoke Tuesday morning, I had a fever, my head hurt, and I was very tired. I stayed in bed for most of Tuesday and Wednesday.

When I awoke on Thursday morning, I still felt bad, so I thought about canceling the ladies meeting, but after I ate breakfast, I felt better, so I went on to the meeting. I was fine during the meeting, but just about the time it ended I began to feel bad again.

That day one of the church ladies had prepared some pumpkin soup and a delicious-looking rice dish for lunch. I didn't have much of an appetite, so when I had eaten about two-thirds of the soup and about half of the rice dish, she noticed that I was just picking at my food. She said, "Pastor, you don't have to force it down." I apologized and left right away. On the way home I was thinking, "That was too bad. She went to all that trouble to prepare the meal, and it looked so delicious, but I just couldn't eat it."

According to the Bible, God has prepared spiritual blessings for our spirit and our soul. In Ephesians 1:3 it says, "Blessed be the God and Father of our Lord Jesus Christ, who hath blessed us with all spiritual blessings." Even though the Lord has prepared wonderful spiritual blessings that surpass our imagination, is our present spiritual condition the kind of condition that can receive those blessings?

Of course we receive many spiritual blessings from the Lord each day, but those are just the tip of the iceberg. Many, many more blessings, both spiritual and material, have been prepared for us, so if our present spiritual condition is not well enough to receive those blessings, this day let's confess our sins to the Lord, receive His forgiveness, and with a clean heart begin to enjoy more and more blessings.

MY TRIBUTE TO
A GREAT MISSIONARY

She never went on deputation. She never received a missionary visa and flew across the seas to witness for Christ. She never studied a foreign language. She never went out on her own and planted a church in a foreign country. But, in my opinion, she was a great missionary.

Who is "she"? She is my mother, who went home to be with the Lord in 2001. Why do I consider her a great missionary? First of all, I consider her to be a great missionary because of the great sacrifice she paid. I realize that it would be sacrilegious to compare any sacrifice of man to the great sacrifice that God paid for us in giving His only Son, but that's exactly what my Mom did. She gave her only child, her only son, for the lost souls of Japan.

Second, I consider her to be a great missionary because of the great attitude she manifested. In spite of the fact that I was her only son, not one time in these thirty-five years did she ever say, "Please don't go to Japan and leave me all alone." In spite of the fact that she knew she would not be able to see her grandchildren (her only grandchildren) for four long years at a time, she never one time pleaded for us not to take her grandchildren all the way to Japan. Instead, she encouraged us, supported us, and she prayed. Oh how she prayed for us!

Finally, in the last year of her life, after physical suffering had brought her much misery and resulted in her being placed in a nursing home, she asked me, "Can't they find someone to take your place?" I didn't answer her question because she and I both already knew the answer. My wife remained in the States to take care of her, but I had to return to Japan.

I admit that I'm prejudiced, but when the Lord hands out the rewards for the ministry in Kyushu, I won't be a bit surprised if He gives one of the biggest rewards of all to a sweet, white-haired lady named Virginia Massie, my mom.

Ken Board

HER LAST SUNDAY

Watching videos of TV programs with my wife could be frustrating at times. Without saying a word she would suddenly get up and leave, so thinking that she was probably going to the bathroom or to the kitchen for a snack, I would pause the video and wait. I would wait several minutes, and when she didn't return, I would go looking for her and find her asleep in bed.

One night she did something she had never done before. We had just finished watching a program when I received a phone call. While I was talking on the phone, she got up out of her chair and headed for the bedroom, but just before she entered the room, she stopped and smiled and waved her hand. That moment has become a precious moment in my memory, for early the next morning she suffered a cerebral hemorrhage and went home to be with the Lord.

The next day I was looking through her Bible and I found two verses that she had written in her own hand. Inside the front cover of her Bible she had written, "Delight thyself also in the Lord; and he shall give thee the desires of thine heart" (Psalm 37:4). Inside the back cover of her Bible she had written, "Be thou faithful unto death, and I will give thee a crown of life" (Revelation 2:10).

"Faithful"—there is no more fitting word to describe the life of Louise Board. To her children she was a faithful mother. To her husband she was a faithful wife. To her Lord she was a faithful servant and missionary. On the last Sunday of her life, she attended church in the morning and went out with the church members to distribute tracts and church flyers in the afternoon. Faithful!

When people speak of us and our last Sunday on this earth, I wonder what they will say.

B-O-A-R-D

(This has nothing to do with the Bible. It's just a comical "routine" that I use to introduce myself at churches. There is a genuine purpose in the routine too. It's my way of helping the members of my supporting churches remember to pray for me.)

My name is Ken Board, and the last name is spelled like a plain old board: B-O-A-R-D. I was born in Roanoke, Virginia, and in that area there are a lot of Boards, but I find that as I travel from church to church, sometimes I am the only guy in town named Board. (Have you seen the car signs that read "Child On Board"? I plan to have one made that reads "Board on Board.")

The pastors of the churches that I visit have a lot of fun with my name. I have been introduced as Brother Wood. I have been introduced as Brother Plank. I have been introduced as Brother Two-by-Four.

I used to complain to the Lord. "Why did I have to be named Board? Why couldn't I have been a Smith or a Jones?" But then I realized that it could have been worse. My name might have been B-O-R-E-D. That would be a terrible name for a preacher. It would be like going up to bat with two strikes already on you.

My first name is Ken, but I don't know why my folks named me Ken. Ken just doesn't go with Board, so I have been introduced many times by such names as Brother Bill Board, Brother Black Board, and Brother White Board. In Charleston, South Carolina, I was introduced as Brother Card Board and in Miami as Brother Surf Board. I appeared on a live TV show in Tyler, Texas, one day and was introduced as Missionary Bulletin Board.

Probably the funniest one of all took place in Cape Girardeau, Missouri. When I walked into the church, there was a large sign on the wall which read, "Welcome, Brother Ken Board." However the word *Brother* was abbreviated without a period and there was very little space between "Brother" and "Ken," so the sign read "Welcome, BroKen Board."

I have four children. When they were small, the people at our home church in Jacksonville, Florida used to call them our "splinters." My wife and I had already picked out the names in case we had a fifth child. If the child were a girl, we were going to call her "Peg," and if the child were a boy, we were going to call him "Ruman."

My family has quite a heritage. In the field of education, School Board has made quite a name for himself. In the world of business and music, Keyboard has been quite successful. In the field of transportation Buckboard, Running Board, and Dashboard have won acclaim. As for sports, what would we do without a Backboard, a Leaderboard, a Diving Board, and a Scoreboard?

In this age of computers I had a Mother Board in my home before most people knew what a computer was.

There is also quite a biblical heritage to my name. When you read the book of Exodus, you will find my ancestors mentioned almost fifty times in connection with the construction of the tabernacle.

It's also possible that one of my relatives saved the life of the apostle Paul. The twenty-seventh chapter of Acts records the sinking of a ship on which Paul was sailing. Included among the methods used by people to make it safely to land, it says "some on boards," so perhaps one of my ancestors helped Paul make it to the shore.

I would like to say that all of my relatives have been above board all across the board, but I am certain all of you have heard of the infamous Deacon Board.

Well, I had better stop now. I think I just went overboard.